GROWING UP LATCHKEY

A Healing Journey from PTSD to Spiritual Awakening

Darla K. Johnson Ph.D.

Foreword by Julie Brown Yau, PhD

BALBOA.
PRESS
A DIVISION OF HAY HOUSE

Balboa Press books may be ordered through booksellers or by contacting:

Balboa Press
A Division of Hay House
1663 Liberty Drive
Bloomington, IN 47403
www.balboapress.com
1 (877) 407-4847

Because of the dynamic nature of the Internet, any web addresses or links contained in this book may have changed since publication and may no longer be valid. The views expressed in this work are solely those of the author and do not necessarily reflect the views of the publisher, and the publisher hereby disclaims any responsibility for them.

The author of this book does not dispense medical advice or prescribe the use of any technique as a form of treatment for physical, emotional, or medical problems without the advice of a physician, either directly or indirectly. The intent of the author is only to offer information of a general nature to help you in your quest for emotional and spiritual well-being. In the event you use any of the information in this book for yourself, which is your constitutional right, the author and the publisher assume no responsibility for your actions.

This book is a work of non-fiction. Unless otherwise noted, the author and the publisher make no explicit guarantees as to the accuracy of the information contained in this book and in some cases, names of people and places have been altered to protect their privacy.

Any people depicted in stock imagery provided by Getty Images are models, and such images are being used for illustrative purposes only. Certain stock imagery © Getty Images.

Print information available on the last page.

ISBN: 978-1-9822-0228-6 (sc)
ISBN: 978-1-9822-0229-3 (e)

Library of Congress Control Number: 2018904423

Balboa Press rev. date: 04/10/2018

To my sons, Zech and Seth, who have made me understand
the true meaning of love, compassion, and forgiveness.
You both have brought me more happiness, love, and pure
joy than I ever thought possible in my life. I cherish and
am proud of every moment of your lives so far. Thank
you both for teaching me from the gifts God gave you
and enriching my life with butterfly kisses, hand-painted
Christmas ornaments, school performances, Nerf and
Airsoft wars, first dates, first proms, graduations, marriages,
and everything in between! The best is yet to come!

To the brave women of the USA Gymnastics Team and
the precious Turpin children; I'm sorry the adults in your
life hurt you and failed you over and over again. #Metoo.
I promise you will go on. You will heal. You are more
than survivors—you are conquerors of the darkness!

Acknowledgments

When I was an impressionable girl of thirteen-years-old old, I decided I wanted to become a psychologist. I was in middle school when I made the excited announcement to my parents that I wanted to "study people's behaviors and especially their psychology—or psyche—that seemingly invisible thread that governs all of our life choices." My very loving and very patient stepfather went out of his way to nurture and support my dreams of one day becoming a "healer of the psyche." He and I would often engage in long conversations way past my bedtime, talking endlessly about human behavior, cognition, unconscious motives, and thought processes. Dad continually challenged me to think outside of the box and logically reason through my inexperienced questions. He challenged me to research psychological concepts and dive into my passion immediately! He would, in all authenticity and love, refer to me as "the psychologist," even to his adult friends.

These seemingly minor role-playing sessions with my stepdad may appear silly as a sensible parenting practice, but as you will see, his love established a foundation of trust, emotional safety, and confidence. Those concepts were foreign to me when he entered my life when I was eleven years old. It took the unwavering, never-failing, never-yielding, unconditional love of a stepfather. Years later, with tears of joy in my eyes and pride beaming from his, we shared a very special moment as he watched his daughter walk across the commencement stage among hundreds to be announced to the world for the first time as "Dr. Darla."

Although I specifically acknowledge and honor my stepdad for being a huge part of what made me the strong woman I am today, I want to especially acknowledge stepparents everywhere. You make a difference in the lives of "other's children." Please never forget how special your role is, especially when others have failed in their roles. I love you Dad … forever.

Ode to the Stepdad

Susan E. Winover

Although you're not my birth dad,
You've loved me since I was small.
The road has not always been easy,
I'm sure at times you've wondered,
How you even got here at all.
There may have been times when I was distant,
Resenting you because you weren't my "real" dad.
And when the going got real rough at times,
I'm sure you felt you'd been had.
But time is the great healer.
She's patient and loving and kind.
One day, I woke up from my slumber,
And with you, I just changed my mind.
I decided you weren't such a bad guy.
You really seemed like you cared.
You seemed to make Mommy so happy.
Perhaps I could open my heart just a wee little bit,
A wee little bit if I dared.
You stood there with arms wide open.

When I decided to take the "chance,"
It seemed so natural and made such sense.
Like a lovely, well-choreographed dance,
You never held it against me.
Those early days when I wasn't so sure,
And when you hold me so close and so dear,
I now know our love is real and pure.

Written for Audrey Rose, by Mommy

I'd like to offer a very special acknowledgement to my developmental trauma therapist, Dr. Julie Brown Yau, PhD. You have been so kind to contribute the foreword to my book. Thank you for being my strength when I had none, believing in me when others did not, and for being my psychological tether to this earth plane and spiritual space holder into greater realms. Most of all, thank you for being a sensitive and compassionate light worker and guide during the dark night of my soul's journey while I found my way back home to myself and divine love within.

Foreword

Many of us will face a time where we feel extremely overwhelmed and where the pain of our existence pushes us to make a change, even if that change takes us to places we have avoided, consciously or unconsciously, our whole lives. This book describes this experience—when the need for courage, perseverance, and healing precedes all else. In any lasting transformation from suffering into aliveness, vibrancy, and joy, this is the journey we need to take.

We cannot fully understand many of the challenges we face in adulthood outside the context of our infant and childhood experiences. For instance, we may have a certain perception about the world that people are not to be trusted or that people hurt us, abandon us, or need us for their own comfort. We then position ourselves in the world as always needing to protect ourselves, which really limits who we are and how we'll be in our relationships. The tendency to be aggressive, arrogant, distant, or incompliant—and the need to please everyone—protects us when we perceive that something terrible will happen to us. The perception is often underneath ordinary awareness. It is not so much about explicit memory—what we readily remember—but how our brains and bodies have adapted to what happens to us and around us. The perceptions become a lens through which we view the world. Until we recognize our distorted views of the world, we believe this is the way life is.

Not everyone will explore their early pasts as a means to heal the pain of their present circumstances or come to know how important the first years of their lives were in forming who they become in adulthood. To live consciously, we owe it to ourselves to explore who we are. The true self is directly connected to the divinity within, and it is often overlaid with false identities, beliefs, and behaviors that emerged when we were young if our environments were unable to provide us with what we needed to feel completely safe and fully connected.

Empathy, mirroring, holding, nurturing, and attunement provided by caregiver typically occur during the first three years of a child's life. They are essential to a child's development of a coherent sense of self, identity, and safety. When these basic needs are lacking, we experience degrees of fear and separation. Without the necessary internal and/or external soothing, a psychobiological state of emotional dysregulation and nervous-system disorganization occurs. These forms of dysregulation significantly and negatively affect personality development, a person's ability to stay connected to their sensations and emotions, express their core needs, and their sense of feeling fully alive. These disruptions or failures of the basic needs in early life, including severe neglect and abuse, create what is commonly referred to under the umbrella term of *developmental trauma*. The outcome is disconnection from ourselves, others, and the world around us.

Developmental trauma, disrupted attachment to our primary caregivers, and early acute traumas often lead to psychological and physiological problems such as anxiety, depression, insomnia, an inability to concentrate, hypertension, intrusive thoughts, heart disease, and addictive and self-destructive behaviors.

As we mature, our infant and childhood memories fade into the further recesses of our minds; some memories are never explicitly remembered. The experiences of fear and separation are hidden in the depth of our psyches and the folds of our brains.

Yet, it is precisely those experiences and memories that can allow us to understand the impact of our early lives and resolve the challenges and difficulties we face later in life.

Without the basic, yet necessary elements of nurturance, attunement, and love, infants and children experience the world as threatening. If environment continues to fail us, and those failures (in the form of caregiving ruptures, acute trauma, or both) are not repaired, our life force energy—our vitality—flows into defenses that help us feel protected. Defenses are automatic protective reactions to cover our pain. For example, if we feel threatened, we may withdraw or try to appease the other person. Yet, these defenses distort who we truly are, and over time, we lose sense of the innate connection to the divine self. It seems that part of the human condition is to experience some wound that creates separation, pain, and fear. A child may feel it is too much to bear and further separate from the self. The experiences of the pain of separation and fear create a negative feedback loop that may last into adulthood. We can break this loop by healing early trauma, and because trauma lives in the body, the body must be included in the process.

Staying connected to the body can be too much to bear without loving support and a sense of safety. Emotions that arise in distressful situations, such as sadness, fear, and anger, can feel intolerable. The inborn defense of dissociation is a gift that allows us to disconnect from ourselves and our feelings for a while. Dissociation is in many ways a lifesaving defense, yet when it becomes a pattern that stays with us, and when we do not receive the loving support that allows us to reconnect, dissociation becomes life denying.

To appreciate and reconcile these erroneous expressions of who we think we are is to also understand that when we are born into an environment that fails to give us the love, nurturance, attunement, and mirroring we need to form healthy, strong notions of self, the defenses numb us from our bodies, and we dissociate, or even fragment, in which thoughts, behaviors, and emotions are split off from our conscious awareness. Restoring our connection to the body is a major part of the healing process, in which we can integrate those split off parts of our sense of wholeness.

As children, when our environments fail us, we tend to blame ourselves with notions that we must not deserve love, that the world is not safe, that our bodies are not safe, that we are not worthy or good enough, that we are inherently bad, and many other erroneous convictions that will sink into the depths of our beings and distort our views and experiences of who we are. Also, if our natural aggressive impulses are ignored or threatened—those that are inherently in place to our alert caregivers that we are in need—they may turn to into anger. As a child, it may not feel safe to express aggression, so we avoid or try to repress those feelings or impulses to survive, and they remain frozen in time. These aspects of being become living, twisted perceptions in our unconscious minds that tear us apart from the inside out. The disparity between these twisted perceptions and the truths of the inner self creates a deep despair. Even if we are not consciously aware of this because of our disconnection, our ability to feel and express our emotions throughout life will be limited.

In adulthood, when we hit a period of deep crisis, we need to be willing to look deep into our psyches to see if any parts of our consciousness—or parts of our selves—have been left behind, waiting for us to bring them back into the light of love and awareness. If we do this, we are more likely to live with authenticity and the full aliveness of our birthright. Not everyone will have the opportunity, the courage, or the perseverance it takes to recognize and begin to heal early trauma; it is not an easy or linear journey. However, it can be a fruitful voyage back into the fullness of life and into knowing ourselves—completely—for the first time.

Darla's book is a spiritual expression of human suffering,

which can be born out of our difficulties in early life, and it is also a demonstration of transcending that suffering. It is a personal journey that reflects how early trauma and a lack of understanding early trauma affect society and culture at large. When we disregard—consciously or unconsciously—the depth of suffering within us, our own needs are desensitized, and so is our ability to recognize the needs of others. Our societal perspectives become distorted, and the fabric of our interconnectedness is torn.

This book has a thoughtful and much-needed message that illustrates why we should not avoid our sadness or pain; if we do so, we decrease our capacity to learn from it. Instead, we should seek the seeds of anguish from which the pain arises so we can heal its roots and be free from the erroneous beliefs that are often the cause of suffering. Because trauma is not a path one should travel alone, a personal journey of healing often begins with a gesture of reaching out to another such as a friend or a therapist. When we reach out, we begin to summon the love and connection that can foster the wonder of healing and growth. Trauma is about disconnection from the self, from God or spirit, and from each other. Resolving trauma is about connection, hope, and love. Hope can be born in the field of intersubjectivity, the shared experience of coming together, with the intention to heal, where solutions and new experiences can replace the old, worn-out, painful ones.

As a trauma therapist, I am frequently asked: How do you work with trauma every day? Isn't it sad and depressing? Well, as you read Darla's story, you may understand why I choose to do this work. As I witness and participate in trauma work with individuals and families, the process is enlivening and heart opening. Of course, I hear stories that sink my heart and bring me great dismay about humanity. Yet, the transformation of the body, mind, and soul, and the expansion of consciousness that occurs among my clients—and in myself as I work with them—is inspiring and uplifting.

The psychic pain of trauma can feel torturous—and so can the healing journey to anyone who embarks upon it. In this process, we are expanding the sphere of our dysregulated boundaries to be able to feel more with less dysregulation and pain. Psychologists call this an increase in consciousness. Because the body and mind are so intimately connected, psychic and body numbness will inevitably lead to harmful physical symptoms of some sort if we don't find a way back to happiness. Increasing consciousness raises the possibility of removing the fear that keeps us bound to our suffering and allows us to emerge from what we once shut down. It is possible to navigate the storms of our psyches when we do not feel alone while expanding our capacity to experience life's myriad challenges.

Ultimately, we realize we were not at fault. There is no question of our worthiness of love; the environment failed to give us the loving and nurturing support we needed. As trauma begins to heal within us, a larger perspective is often revealed in which we also no longer blame those who were not able to support us as we needed—or those who hurt us.

Post-Traumatic Growth

Another inspiring element of working in the field of trauma therapy is that research has shown us we can emerge from life's traumas and trauma symptoms psychologically and psychobiologically healthier than we were before the trauma. This growth, known as *post-traumatic growth*, is beautifully paradoxical because it can occur simultaneously to trauma symptoms or post-traumatic stress disorder. As we suffer, we can also grow and enhance our capacities for conscious awareness. With post-traumatic growth, some individuals emerge from life's challenges feeling healthier and have a greater sense of agency—feeling more competent, upright, and self-reliant—and as such, they can accept their humanness in its multifaceted expression, their relationships can become deeper and more meaningful, and their spiritual beliefs expand and strengthen. This kind of growth leads to a deeper appreciation of life itself.

For some individuals, like Darla, trauma began so early that existence without some form of internalized threat or fear was unknown to her. Darla's journey is an uplifting expression of post-traumatic growth and the strength of the human spirit. She explicitly shows how finding relational resources, accepting what happened so as not to feel like a victim, and perseverance are vital components of post-traumatic growth. Through our sessions together and disciplined meditative practices, she began to shift the functioning of her brain to be able to feel and continue to cultivate positive emotions, which also shifted her moods and behavior. Ultimately, she could harness power to choose how she related to the traumatic events of her life and how she perceived herself in relation to them. A cohesive story about her life emerged, bringing with it compassion, aliveness, and a more inclusive sense of spirituality.

Effects of Child Care and Trauma

Darla's trauma began when she was very young, likely while developing in the womb of her very frightened, and not well supported, sixteen-year-old mother. Research tells us that if a pregnant mother is in a highly dysregulated state, cortisol passes through the placenta in utero, which negatively affects the structures that are evolving in the brain of the fetus. The biological distress of the mother creates distress in the fetus, which is held in implicit memory in the core of the infant's experience. Even at this very early stage of life, the fetus will go into withdrawal state when there is persistent distress. Later in life, the child may be highly prone to dissociation, which is an indicator of whether a person will go on to experience traumatic stress. The underlying biological stress is at the foundation of psychological distress. When Darla was born, she was adopted by a family who tragically were not able to give her the love and attention she needed. Very often, adoption creates many challenges for the child, even when the adoptive family is very loving and supportive.

It has only been over the past few decades that neuroscience has informed us that in infancy and childhood, when the morphology and functioning of brain and body systems are being established, infants are malleable and responsive to their early experiences. Through the research of object relations and developmental and attachment theories, we now understand that love, attunement, mirroring, nurturing, and nourishment are vital elements for a child's survival, flourishing, psychological well-being, and overall well-being. Sadly, current culturally derived child-rearing practices still advocate some false truths, such as leaving infants and toddlers to children to cry for long periods without caring intervention. As such, infants and adults continue to suffer.

Darla speaks to the era of latchkey children and the detrimental effects of leaving young children alone while the parents work. Let's take a look at an even earlier period from which deleterious child-rearing practices influenced generations. In 1928, leading American behaviorist John B. Watson published *Psychological Care of Infant and Child*. The underlying philosophy of this book suggested that the nurturance and love a mother provided for her children would ruin and spoil them. In other words, Watson suggested that love and affection were inevitably dangerous and would make for weak human beings. Imagine the mothers of that generation feeling the overpowering instinct to want to comfort their children but being afraid to do so for fear of "ruining" them. Unfortunately, this book became a best seller throughout the United States, and many parents, pediatricians, and medical institutions subscribed to the recommendation that children should not be picked up when they cry. Cuddling, nurturing, attuning, and expressions of love and affection were largely considered unnecessary at best and detrimental at worst. Even today, there are remnants of this tragic lack of understanding—passed down from one generation to another—of an infant's most fundamental emotional and physical needs. The notion of leaving an infant to "cry it out" is still a common practice recommended by pediatricians. Yet neurosciences confirm that letting babies get distressed is a custom that can harm children and their long-term relational capacities. A child left to cry it out is more likely to be anxious, awkward, less intelligent, less healthy, and can pass these traits on to the next generation.

There is now an abundance of research corroborating that loving and attentive support in infant and child development establishes positive qualities that shape a child's empathy, compassion, tolerance, and resilience as well as the capacity to live well with uncertainty. During early childhood, it is the modulation of the child's emotional states, provided by the primary caregivers, whose caring interventions influence the child's brain for self-regulation and emotional regulation. This also promotes confidence and mental health along with establishing healthy emotional patterns that are important for well-being throughout life.

Loving interventions allow a child to learn that negative emotions are tolerable, that they won't last forever, and that relational stress can be calmed. In other words, they learn that the world will feel safe again after distress. The primary caregivers help the child down-regulate what are thought of as negative emotions, emotions that feel distressing, and up-regulate positive emotions, such as joy and happiness. To live a full, abundant, and relational life, we need to be able to tolerate the entire spectrum of emotions.

The imprinting of positive interventions allows us to tolerate stress and helps us tolerate stress and mitigate the negative effects of trauma in adulthood. Conversely, adverse child-rearing practices, including insufficient holding, attunement, attachment, and mirroring, are thought to shape negative character traits, limiting children's ability to experience compassion, empathy, and interconnectedness. Without these essential elements of caregiving, a child experiences a sense of undefinable threat. For instance, leaving a child unattended when he or she is in distress signals to his or her body that danger is imminent, which may lead to withdrawal, shutdown, and dissociation. Research has shown that an infant's brain is flooded with high levels of potentially neurotoxic stress hormones when left alone to cry without timely intervention.

There are also serious physical consequences for a child who experiences dissociation, including dysregulation in important systems that oversee health, such as the endocrine, nervous, vascular, and digestive systems, leaving the child vulnerable to many diseases and health issues throughout life, including the epigenetically altered function of the immune system. Often, individuals have little awareness of their severe disconnection from their physical selves, and they live life through the distorted lens of unresolved trauma and an arrested development of various important stages of mental and emotional growth. The dissociative process imparts profound suffering, diminishment of a sense of vibrancy and aliveness, a collapse of our sense of self, disconnection to others, and a multitude of physical compromises.

The collapse of the implicit self is signaled by the intensification of deep emotions like anger, shame, and disgust and by feelings of hopelessness and helplessness. The rupture of *intersubjectivity*—the field between the caregiver and child— often leads to an instant dissipation of safety and trust that we can carry with us throughout life. Recent studies have shown that infants' and children's exposure to interpersonal traumatic stressors is exceedingly common, and the resulting trauma has been described by many experts in the field as a silent epidemic.

Through the continued neglect of infants' and children's primary emotional and social needs, Western society may be normalizing deviations in healthy caregiving. A considerable amount of interpersonal trauma might be avoided with careful education and support for parents and caregivers and a shift in the current cultural milieu on how children are treated. Practices such as extended periods of attachment, bonding through social engagement, breastfeeding, parent-like behavior toward an infant who is not one's offspring, longer periods of attunement with greater awareness of repairing ruptures in attunement, and co-sleeping can diminish the likelihood of developmental trauma and the corresponding negative results.

Healing Our Deepest Wounds

Neuroscientifically informed practices that incorporate the body and mind can assist in overcoming the unpredictable challenges that unresolved early trauma can bring in adulthood. Research has observed that the brain continually adapts to new conditions, and its plasticity remains throughout a lifetime, modifying its patterns of connection among different regions of the brain while reorganizing neural pathways and functions as well as developing new neurons. The brain influences humans' thinking, feeling, speaking, and acting in ways that either keep them habituated to certain behaviors or set them free. Many practices used today for the resolution of trauma are drawn from ancient wisdom traditions and adapted by contemporary neuroscience for the explicit purpose of building new neural pathways that become the basis for behavioral changes and improvements in people's lives.

Trauma is an intrinsically biological phenomenon, and healing or resolving trauma needs, as I mentioned earlier, to include the body. By observing inner sensations, emotions, and thoughts, we can realize that our internal landscapes change. Thus, we can cultivate influence over physiological states and actively affect the trajectory of the mind. This capability offers significant hope for those who have suffered trauma encompassing neglect, abuse, and post-traumatic stress disorder.

You are not alone in your desire to identify the obstacles that stand in the way of your psychological and spiritual growth and learn how to release them from the deepest core places in your psyche and body. The gift of Darla's book is that she is living evidence of someone who has reached her desired destination of living life freely, abundantly, and without being tethered to the limitations of her past beliefs. Her journey of healing may still continue, but the crux of her anguish was met and resolved. Despite continuing and repeated trauma and feelings of hopelessness and despair, there comes a time when the need for courage, perseverance, and healing precedes all else. We need only begin.

—Dr. Julie Brown Yau, PhD

Introduction

This is not the story I necessarily wanted to tell or the story I had dreamed of all my life. I had no idea this would become the story that would birth my magnum opus—my great work—my own unique contribution to the world of post-trauma sufferers, desperately seeking comfort and relief, to offer psychological wisdom as a healing practitioner. Those intentions alone drove and steered my entire life—to bring ease to the suffering and heal the brokenhearted. Little did I realize my offering to the world would tell my life story and of a lifetime of suffering. Like so many in the world, my drive to offer hope and healing would be born out of my own utter brokenhearted-ness that ultimately shattered my spirit beginning in childhood from profound parental neglect and sibling abuse growing up in middle class America in the sixties, seventies, and eighties.

It is amazing to me how, seemingly overnight, your whole life can be uprooted and altered forever by an event in your adult life that would begin to awaken those dark memories and force you to look far back over the course of your life to the roots in childhood. I had a realization that the very defense mechanisms that I had so skillfully developed since childhood—out of a desperate need for safety and survival—had actually grown into a twisted and dark tree of toxic and skewed perceptions of reality and life.

For me, coming to terms with my traumatic childhood was like waking up from an unconscious nightmare. And like so many of the clients I had counseled as a psychotherapist, I awoke to the fact that I too had become adept at repressing terrifying memories. In the end, life would end up rendering me utterly paralyzed in mind/body/spirit until I came to terms with my past unresolved trauma to eventually, and gracefully, lead me into a great spiritual awakening and understanding about the true nature of reality, finally ending years of suffering and beginning my trauma healing journey and post-trauma growth. The very childhood trauma curse that loomed over me all my life, when finally faced head-on, would turn out to be the most miraculous blessing encompassing the most personal and professional growth I could have ever imagined. The healing journey set in motion miraculous cosmic synchronicities in which my inner and outer life began to align and come together in complete harmony that changed the course of my life forevermore.

But before the blessings came the journey deep into my trauma hell. I would experience what is referred to by mystics and poets across the ages as "the dark night of the soul" on my hero's journey, but I would eventually arise spiritually transformed by an unseen alchemy in mind, body, and spirit of such magnitude that I had never experienced in all my years in organized religion or the Western-trained psychology, medicine and behavioral neurosciences. This awakened state of consciousness dropped me into a place of profound awareness seeing the oneness and divinity within everything.

The power of Divine Universal love transformed, revealed, and healed my inner child's broken heart and spirit. Love, the only power that can awaken us all to the true nature of reality, revealing who we really are and have been since the dawn of time, from the incarnation of our souls on this earth. Revealing that all I had previously understood as reality through social conditioning of parents, teachers, friends, employers, higher education, governments, and organized religion would ultimately be shattered along my journey through the dark night of my soul. All former belief systems I held were revealed to me as mere illusions I created and defended so fiercely. This experience deep into the psychic underworld and back would radically shift my perceptions from a mere *believer* to a direct *experiencer* as understood by mystics and sages of old. The Noetic traditions of "knowing" firsthand what you and I are made of by the cosmos is a place where the soul leaves off all social conditioning to journey into an unchartered landscape of silent understanding of the true nature of reality and of the soul's purpose of being on this earth.

Ever since I was a child, I have been deeply intuitive, empathic, and drawn to anything spiritual. I developed a sense to feel the location of individuals I focused on, and I could fully understand their feelings and perceive their thoughts at times. We all have this intuitive sixth sense, but mine was developed and strengthened out of a need for emotional and psychological survival as a child. Years later in my advanced training and work as a therapist, I realized that many survivors of childhood neglect and abuse, out of sheer necessity, have the highest percentage of developing this subtle intuitive energy, accurately reading their physical and emotional environments to quickly determine the level of physical and emotional threat. Survivors of developmental trauma become very adept and keen at threat assessment. Tragically however, the same heightened and well-developed intuition that offered protections as a small child later on often becomes psychologically distorted morphing into a post-trauma hyperarousal state. Unresolved trauma energies become locked within the body's central and enteric nervous systems, which imprison the psyche until processed, repaired and released in the body.

At the beginning of my own trauma healing and transformation three years ago, I began to understand that, on this next path of my life's journey, all my years of higher education and psychological training would not serve to guide me at all. I had to journey deep into years of my own repressed childhood memories, which were buried deep within my subconscious. It would be the most terrifying journey I would ever encounter. During my trauma therapy, my body would violently shudder and shake involuntarily with each painful step down, down, down into the dark abyss of my subconscious. With each recalled torture, molestation and abuse, my body would vomit up the painful memories, and my central nervous system would begin to tingle like violent electrical shocks while releasing the frozen trauma body memories long trapped and unprocessed. As fought the darkness and the demons, my spiritual eyes began to slowly adjust and come into focus where I could *see* the psychological chains that had kept me bound for so many years. And when life forced me to finally stop running and playing hide-and-seek with my unresolved childhood traumas, I could finally *see* the invisible prison bars I had built around my heart for decades.

If I thought it was hell going down deep into my subconscious, what awaited me there completely undid me. The real work was ahead of me. I had to force open the demon-guarded, doubled-locked steel door that was the entrance between the two worlds of my conscious awareness and repressed unconscious memories in order open the prison doors around my heart and make room for healing and the post-traumatic growth to start to blossom. Little did I realize that this confrontation of my thought-formed demons that began in childhood would summon up the deepest, blackest, most vile terrors hidden in my frozen, childlike heart within. It was the result of over thirteen years of profound parental neglect, sibling and stranger abuses you will read in the pages that follow. The unhealed trauma energies that were frozen in time in my mind and body would send lightning bolts of flashbacks with frightening and overwhelming images and experiencing sheer terror. The bodily trauma information contained within my very being jolted my nervous system throughout my brain and body. Once again, I finally allowed the subconscious, frozen-in-time post-trauma information to start thawing in my body and come forth to be processed after all these years.

As mentioned in the foreword, neuroscience has shown that we all contain biological information that is recorded in our cellular memories—not just in our brains. I term this body-based information the *bio-code*, and it is always recording in our central, peripheral, and enteric nervous systems as Dr. Bessel Van der Kolk M.D. brilliantly outlines in his book *The Body Keeps The Score; Brain, Mind and Body in The Healing of Trauma.*

The bio-code for trauma survivors also contains a hidden *trauma-response code program* that is waiting to be activated. This bodily response with its cluster of associated behavior is commonly referred to as post-traumatic stress disorder (PTSD). I would like to offer a more accurate description when referring to bodily and behavioral trauma reactions as a post-traumatic stress response (PTSR) rather than the stigmatized idea of a "disorder". Unconscious trauma information comes forth as a bodily response when triggered by what we perceive as overwhelming feelings of soul annihilation or physical threats whether real or imaginal.

The brain is a powerful, mysterious, and magnificent organ. I particularly fell in love with the brain early in my graduate studies and medical training in health psychology and behavioral neuroscience. This powerful control center contains more than 100 billion neural synaptic connections that are capable of processing unquantifiable bits of information throughout our bodily systems in nanoseconds. In addition to processing and sorting enormous amounts of incoming sensory information the brain's prime directive for executing the appropriate cognitive and behavioral responses or *root genetic bio-code* as I term it, is for the survival and homeostasis of the organism—by *any* means.

As I remind students of behavioral neuroscience, the magnificent brain, as we all no doubt have experienced, can be friend or foe, bully or encourager, angel or devil. Behavioral neuroscientists and neuropsychologists understand that—well beyond the biological structure and function of the brain—lies the mysterious interface between matter and spirit, between the realms of mere reductionist materialism into the largely unexplained areas of the subconscious. C. G. Jung and Sigmund Freud were among the first psychotherapists to explore the mysterious realms of the subconscious brain among the numerous patients they worked with and detailed their psychoanalytic findings in an impressive body of work they left behind within several peer-reviewed journal articles and books. I've heard many presentations from current physicists of today who seem to be supporting the notion that each cell in our body even contains a quantum world of conscious activity that perhaps stores lifelong memories throughout our entire body system and not just within our psyche or physical brains. Moreover, trauma memories appear to go beyond even the body/brain connection to the meta-physical netherworlds deep within our soul or our "emotional body". The body/brain is therefore like a receiver that simply helps us regulate our bodily systems and our emotions at the cellular level.

In the case of a child who is neglected, abused, or traumatized, this information stays deep in the body memory and gets distorted. It can create emotional dysregulation, hyperarousal, disassociation of self, and irrational fears that last a lifetime if not processed, repaired, and healed. But again, the psyche's prime directive is the survival of the species as all costs and this prime directive is always running in the subconscious as a type of primitive bio-code. Your psyche therefore becomes your ardent protector (or taskmaster) of what it perceives as reality in order to keep you, the organism, alive and in a constant state of psychological homeostasis.

But when a child experiences emotional or physical trauma, their brain structure is permanently altered. For the meme "neurons that fire together, wire together" has been revealed in neuroimaging studies of traumatized brains. These structural changes in the brain due to trauma as a child gives rise to different neuronal pathways of information normally sent to the brain and body, permanently altering the adult's perception of reality as they grow into adulthood. The altered psyche subsequently becomes a "master illusionist", if you will, for the protection and survival of the organism by compelling the individual to start using maladaptive coping mechanisms such as profound psychological repressions tactics thus keeping at bay any horrific and uncomfortable memories of shock or trauma still stored in the body that occurred during childhood in order to maintain psychological homeostasis across the remaining life span.

In addition, if the body memory detects the presence of any current past trauma *feelings*, the brain will protect the organism at all costs by removing the individual from the scene or by succumbing to a full-blown post-traumatic, out-of-control response if the trauma memory takes over the body. Put another way, from a skewed perception of reality created in a child's mind by abuse or neglect, they tend to *act out* at a very primal visceral level, unable to control their outbursts or emotionally regulate themselves. For the PTSD sufferer the body/mind is always on high alert, and the psyche strives to be on lockdown, acting as a gatekeeper to the underworld of the soul's pain. Sometimes, the body takes over fully before the rational brain can rein it in with overwhelming feelings of terror or annihilation. In other words, a sufferer of PTSD cannot consciously control the response once they start ramping up and spinning out into the post-trauma bodily response zone.

Once the body/mind is triggered, there is no going back until the trauma energies are *released* and have essentially run their course throughout the central nervous system and have burned themselves out. Only then can the individual return to physical, cognitive, and emotional homeostasis with rational thought. This is what it is like to live every day with PTSD. And when an attack hits and until the mind/body can regain homeostasis, sadly the irrational behavioral response can leave a wake of shock and awe among its witnesses be they friends or family. It is for this reason that sufferers of PTSD become socially isolated because they are well aware of the fact that their trauma laden outbursts will not be understood or worse, severely judged. And one never knows exactly when a trigger will set off the trauma response so one is left trapped in their own body, prisoners of their psyche. For this reason, social isolation and suicides among the veterans and childhood trauma survivors remain constant in staggering numbers.

The adult child of neglect or abuse lives only to avoid daily triggers—even if done so subconsciously. Triggers for a veteran, as you can imagine, tend to differ greatly from triggers that stem from developmental trauma. Furthermore, triggers of profound neglect (e.g. being left alone for large periods of time compounded with a lack of nurturing by a caregiver) coupled with physical and/or sexual abuse produces what is known as *complex PTSD* or *c*PTSD. It would stand to reason then that an individual surviving child neglect and or/abuse would go on to develop an unconscious *trigger* in which they perceive situations reminiscent of their terrifying days of profound loneliness or abuse. This could involve friends or family members who are perceived as removing their love, attention, or affection. A trigger could also involve a misperception that a store clerk is being exceptionally rude when just stating a fact which might set off a cascade of irrational cognitive and behavioral responses leaving the store clerk with eyes wide open at the c-PTSD response. It's a no-win situation for the adult child of developmental neglect and abuse. Developmental PTSD or c-PTSD leaves an individual with a subtle feeling that you can get close—but not too close to others. You can care—but not too much, for that is where their comfort zone is having known no other way growing up. So, "we" live on an alternate plane of reality daily vacillating between torment and isolation. Pushing people away and alienating others with harsh post-trauma responses no one understands, let alone has compassion for. Paradoxically still yearning and longing for closeness with others that tends to be allusive throughout the life span.

Children of neglect and abuse are therefore left with feelings of complete disconnection from others in their world. They live in a psychological state resembling that of their childhood maltreatment. They have feelings of profound emptiness and even unprocessed rage that surfaces at the most *inconvenient* times. Unfortunately, the repressed childhood anger can be spewed out in the form of irrational or immature thinking and cruelty toward the ones they love the most. Breaking through the deep psychological barrier, many of us try so hard to keep from exposing our childhood maltreatment and its subsequent post-trauma effects.

Traumatized children's minds and bodies become disassociated or disconnected. They slowly lose the ability to *feel* their bodies, and eventually learn to live "in their heads". Many, like myself, pursue careers that demand great intellectual discipline in order to keep from feeling. Disassociation and separation from the head and the body is a common issue among victims of trauma since the body has been a place of terror for years. So in the process of trauma therapy the therapist must work to help the sufferer reintegrate and fully embody the mind and body as one. In other words, when a child or teen has experienced acute or chronic trauma, there is a splitting off of the psyche. A part of the self or vital life force begins to protect the person from body memory terrors endured in childhood. By disassociating and partitioning the memories from the logical mind—keeping it separate from repressed body trauma memory—the mind can transform reality by creating a psychological veil between the subconscious and conscious awareness. This veil or mind illusion has been understood for centuries in the Hindu and Tibetans traditions and referred to as Maya, the trickster or twister of reality. Whether trauma-based or mere social conditioning, this illusory veil gives birth to the ego or false persona in order to defend the individual from what is perceived as a threat to selfhood. It imprisons the sufferer in a false reality, disconnected and disassociated from the true self as well as the body. Maya can veil the traumatized mind and body to bury it deep within the subconscious robbing the unawakened mind and heart to live to its fullest, stifling the reality of the authentic self.

Trauma memory dislodges and separates even the mind from the heart center. This is understandable given the fact that a child who had to endure years of neglect or abuse has endured years of brokenhearted living. It is therefore far easier to partition the broken heart from the affairs of daily living. Children learn to repress the terrors stored in the memories of their bodies about what had *really* been done to them. The purpose of trauma therapy, therefore, is to work with a skilled expert gently titrating the individual back into their body in order to bring back the disassociated emotions and split off parts of the self that were so violently blown apart in childhood and to help the person love, accept and welcome back feelings of loneliness and separation to fully integrate the subtle energies that were partitioned off and alienated from themselves in childhood to ultimately fully integrate all parts of the original and authentic self.

According to the current *Diagnostic and Statistical Manual* (DSM-5) criterion for PTSD symptomology, there is a litany (A-H) of requirements for presentation of behaviors in order for and individual to be diagnosed. Requirements include, but are not limited to, "direct trauma-related arousal, avoidance of similar trauma-related stimuli, isolation, recurrent negative or threatening thoughts, flashbacks, night terrors, night sweats, and hypervigilance". For the first time, the *DSM* also gives credence to pediatric PTSD in children six and under by allowing for its own category, criterion, and requirements for diagnosis.

Readers may be surprised to learn that post traumatic stress disorder has only been recognized as a specific cluster of behavioral responses in the West since 1980—even though trauma has been experienced since the dawn of time. Thankfully, since the 1980s, there have been numerous revisions of the *DSM*. It is moving away from an overly simplistic external event-only model and includes a more subjective validation of how the trauma is perceived at the level of the individual. For example, no two individuals will perceive a car accident and the resulting trauma in the same way. Every person perceives a traumatic event differently; likewise, every PTSD trigger and manifestation (i.e. PTSD attack) for that person will be different as well. Likewise, as mentioned prior, combat veterans experiencing the trauma of war have different triggers and manifest different responses than that of a post-trauma reaction experienced by a person who has untreated childhood trauma, which can essentially be attributed to "the war from childhood."

Furthermore, according to the US Department of Veteran Affairs,

> The latest revision, the DSM-5 (2013), has made a number of notable evidence-based revisions to PTSD diagnostic criteria, with both important conceptual and clinical implications. First, because it has become apparent that PTSD is not just a fear-based anxiety disorder (as explicated in both DSM-III and DSM-IV), PTSD in DSM-5 has expanded to include anhedonic/ dysphoric presentations, which are most prominent. Such presentations are marked by negative cognitions and mood states as well as disruptive (e.g. angry, impulsive, reckless and self-destructive) behavioral symptoms. As a result of research-based changes to the diagnosis, PTSD is no longer categorized as an Anxiety Disorder. PTSD is now classified in a new category, "Trauma- and Stressor-Related Disorders, in which the onset of every disorder has been preceded by exposure to a traumatic or otherwise adverse environmental event." (www.ptsd.va.gov)

The Veteran's Administration (VA) has been on the forefront in the research and advancement of vet-related PTSD diagnosis and treatment since World War I. Thanks to the fine joint cooperative work between the American Psychiatric Association (APA), the American Psychological Association (APA), and the VA's ongoing dedication and commitment to helping suffering veterans cope with the many complex challenges involved with managing post-trauma responses, American society has seen a marked reduction in PTSD-related suicides in the veteran population since the 1980s.

I was reminded of the epidemic still plaguing soldiers however when I came across a YouTube channel that showed thirty-one-year-old Hannah Campbell on the reality show "The Island." The former army corporal from Northampton, England, become one of the few contestants to have been evacuated due to a full-blown PTSD event. I saw her terror ramping up after a benign electric storm came over the island and my own body started to tense as I personally related to her failed attempts at trying to calm her body and talk herself out of a full blown attack. To no avail. As she furiously attempted to manage her spiraling symptoms and bring her spinning central nervous system under control by repeats of rapid swallowing and deep breathing strategies the menacing symptoms of PTSD finally overwhelmed her mind and body, finally and completely engulfing her in a full-blown attack that lasted until dawn and the flight off the island. My heart went out to this amazing and brave woman. I empathized greatly and was very thankful she had loving supportive cast mates who saw her great distress and through the attack until they helped her get off the island to where her body and mind felt safe.

Thankfully, vets now receive far more support and treatment to manage their post-traumatic stress triggers and attacks. Catching the symptoms early is vital for treatment. Vets are required to report to a military therapist for mental health evaluation upon returning home from war or for separation processing from the service in which a majority of veteran PTSD symptomology can be diagnosed where supportive treatment can begin.

There is sadly no such required screening process for evaluation of the overwhelming number of individuals in the civilian population around the world who are adult survivors of childhood neglect and abuse. According to Veteran trauma expert, Dr. Bessel Van der Kolk M.D., for every veteran that suffers from PTSD there are 6-10 adult survivors of childhood abuse/neglect that are living today in torment. This greatly underserved PTSD and c-PTSD population has gone undiagnosed and untreated for years. Despite the fact they are largely untreated, many have gone on to become successful adults. For many of us, we believe that success is measured by how well we can build a life around *successfully managing our symptoms and staying away from known triggers.* For what if an unexpected trigger presents itself and "outs us" in front of an employer demonstrating a full-blown PTSD event—like Hannah Campbell? Many have lost jobs or careers over such events. People who do not understand trauma-related behaviors can judge or label sufferers, making their own guilt and shame unbearable with increased negative internal dialogue.

There was a point in my own life that I hit a wall and came to the stark realization, like so many I have counseled over the years, that I too had unsuccessfully tried to repress my horribly neglectful, lonely and abusive childhood since I left home at seventeen years old. I believed the societal myth that what happens in childhood has little bearing on adult life. Like so many who sought me out for counseling, I also began to *see* my own personal and professional life starting to slowly deteriorate as a result of my unresolved trauma and irrational responses. I fell into the psychological trap that so many of my clients had fallen into and could not find their way out of. They would talk to me about relationship problems, parenting problems, workplace issues, substance abuse, and anger-management problems. Inevitably, during my assessments, observations, and sessions, child maltreatment in one form or another was a common theme in every case.

I recall working with a highly intelligent and successful gentleman who told me after several sessions, with tears in his eyes, that the first time he ever heard his mother say "I love you" was when he was forty-four years old! In another case, I worked with an elementary school teacher who had to always emotionally prepare for our sessions with a few drinks for "liquid courage." One time, he began weeping for all his students who he perceived were "so neglected by parents and hurting." He wanted to "take them all home." As I gently pressed into his past—suspecting projecting of his own upbringing—he also revealed a childhood of profound parental neglect and lack of love and nurturance that little ones so desperately require to grow into health, well-adjusted adults. After working with him for months he would eventually come to an understanding and full agreement that his longing to "save his classroom children" stemmed from seeing himself as a child within the little ones he taught who subconsciously triggered his own unresolved childhood pain. He was also emotionally dying a little each day due to the unresolved childhood trauma that still resided in his heart, mind and body that compelled this poor tormented man to self-medicate with alcohol, which in turn drove his two preteen daughters away from him as they wanted little to do with dad in this state. He loved them so much and because he was divorced, they decided to ration time spent with him for their own mental health. They implored him to seek help for his alcohol addiction but little did they know the seeds of his substance abuse went far deeper that were planted in his childhood upbringing. It is vital to understand that this is the trap and prison of unresolved childhood trauma. PTSD behaviors often result in substance abuse and carry over into our adult lives by affect our relationships with our friends and family. This is why it's vital to have the courage to reach out and start your healing process with a trauma expert as soon as possible.

Another case that stands out in my mind was when I spent months working with a nuclear scientist who had her PhD and was working at a prestigious corporation. She was heartbroken and wept while she told me that she still cannot earn her father's love even after all she has achieved in life. Despite all her success and achievements, she felt the sting of emotional pain and the void left from her father's lack of expressed love for her since childhood. This deep feeling of a lack of being loved by her father consumed her thoughts and overshadowed her entire emotional life. It eventually debilitated and distorted her view of her own self-worth, incredible achievements and undermined her sense of well-being. Biological responses to a lack of expressed love (neglect) and emotional abuse—even in adulthood—create a negative neural feedback loop in which oftentimes, the suffering individual drifts between depression, low self-esteem, and suppressing the emotional trauma. When triggered, the trauma response begins to surface and is replayed over and over again. Many individuals such as these cases turn to prescription drugs or alcohol to relieve the emotional pain.

During the latchkey years many babies were left to "cry it out" alone in their cribs under the false and extremely harmful notion that it is okay to let babies cry themselves to sleep without the mothers' natural instincts and response to comfort their child. Many children of the latchkey generation, due to the misinformation of child rearing practices of the day, knew little nurturing or comfort and through classical conditioning learned to shut down emotionally as they were conditioned no one was coming to comfort them. This is classical stimulus-response (or non-response) conditioning that has been repeated time and time again in the laboratory with dogs, rats, mice and other animals. This same stimulus-response mechanism is present within all of us. This is how fears and phobias develop. When a person experiences a negative *association* with a terrifying event or situation (stimulus) that develops into a fear or phobia (response).

Children are exposed to all sorts of stimuli, negative and positive but when they are subject to associating their emotional needs will not be met no matter how much they cry and scream, they shut down and numb out whereby dissociative behaviors begin.

Developmental trauma(s) cause a profound breach in the bond between parent and child. Clinically, this often results in *relational attachment deficits* or *reactive attachment disorder (RAD)*. This is so important to understand because the unmet emotional and psychological needs of a child in the formative years of development does not allow for the child to *learn* to attach at any individual at the emotional level (classical conditioning once again). Many criminal behaviors have been directly traced back to *attachment disorders* with a lack of emotional or psychosocial attachment, care, or compassion for another human being, typically learned in childhood. This is why neglect, which is a parent or caregiver not meeting the emotional and psychological needs of a child, is stated as "the most insidious form of child maltreatment even if not apparent abuse," according to the National Institute of Mental Health (NIMH).

When a child does not receive the appropriate love, attention, and affection for normal development, an emotional disconnect develops. This is because children derive their sense of identity and well-being most importantly their connection to others from the direct reflection of their parents. At the most fundamental level of child psychology, science has repeatedly shown that the neglected child is classically conditioned by the parent(s) to form unhealthy attachments that affect all other future relationships. The treatment therefore, for child neglect is distinct, as you shall see, from the treatment of child trauma. Big Pharma could never touch what ailed me—a broken heart and spirit. I came to realize however that I had to take responsibility and be accountable for my own mental health and personal growth if I wanted to be happy and free of past conditioning.

However, there is great news for survivors of parental neglect and developmental trauma. There have been many breakthroughs in trauma therapy and research to support individuals in setting themselves free from this seemingly never-ending pattern of self-torture, depression, and repression. If you commit to your own mental and physical health and take care to do the hard work, I promise you will achieve the sought-after "peace that passeth understanding" you so desperately seek and deserve. My own recovery bears witness to this fact. Although life does not magically become perfect, the self-torture will cease and you will finally gain inner peace in your heart and mind. I learned to successfully welcome home those long-alienated and previously denied parts of myself by learning to have great compassion on myself each day and where I learned to stop judging myself so harshly to finally mend a little girl's broken heart and fractured spirit welcoming the birth and blossoming of my long hidden authentic self.

After trauma therapy, for the first time in my life, my soul felt safe and I finally felt at home in my own body. I no longer feel like an alien in this world or long to be free of it. The transformation on my particular healing journey also included two life transforming out-of-body experiences (OBE) that changed my life forever. I am no longer afraid of death and no longer seek ambition or status. I also ceased in tirelessly pushing myself to overachieve or over please others. Each day, I am freer than the day before. What an amazing journey of trauma healing it has been. Beyond knowing in my head, I now *feel* in my body that the neglect and abuse I endured growing up during the latchkey era, along with many others of this neglected generation, no longer define me or control me.

For me, the greatest lesson I was shown through my trauma treatment, OBE, and awakening was that we are all spiritual beings having a human experience on this earth. We are here to learn how to love ourselves, forgive, and love all other beings. I learned this by processing all of the abuses inflicted on my body as a little girl, as well as having an experience of massive empathy and profound grief for the pain daily inflicted on all the children of this planet who are neglected, abused, starving, or victims of warmongering. When I came through this dark and painful journey I was finally able to let go by *de-identifying* from my old story and moved into my true authentic self, free from past human atrocities inflicted on me. I allowed myself to come home to the full divine essence of who I am--to be fully awakened. I am beginning a new, fully transformed life and lifestyle—and you can as well. Global consciousness is awakening everywhere.

It has been a long five decades to get to this point in my life. In this book, you may begin to understand the many reasons why many sufferers of PTSD tend to avoid entertaining the idea of revisiting the demons of their past by seeking out therapy as adults. Perhaps you will also begin to empathize a little more with your fellow sojourner on this planet and gain a new sense of compassion. Not even trained professionals in mental health truly understand anyone else's internal pain or struggles but we all can be a little less judgmental and more compassionate regardless. Those who struggle and spend lifetimes repressing and running from childhood nightmares are not quick to invite back the terror to relive and process these experiences. However, for any quality of life or to gain freedom within our souls to live authentic lives, it must be so.

So it was after a year of specialized somatic-based trauma therapy—drawn from much of the work pioneered by trauma experts Dr. Peter Levine M.D. and Dr. Bessel Van der Kolk M.D.—I was able to admit to myself the enormous negative impact that a childhood of profound neglect and abuse really had affected my entire adult life. Like so many sufferers it had subconsciously dictated many of my behaviors and decisions later in life until it culminated in finally losing all that I loved, a final blow of heartbreak that finally caused me to stop running, denying, and repressing my past. It was only then that I completely surrendered and found the Love I had sensed in innocent childhood—before my innocence was so violently taken from me. I was out of strength, out of faith, and out of time. So, with toe-in-the-water shakiness, I would—for the first time—trust another being on this planet with my heart and mind, asking for help in finding my lost self, my dissociated life force, and my shut-down, innocent childlike heart.

When I finally faced my past, I began to experience heaven and earth beginning to align, or should I say my heart and mind. Many miraculous synchronicities began following and assisting me in my healing process. After a complete loss of everything I held dear and decades of living with flashbacks, night terrors, and thought form-created demons, I was guided to specific and expert gentle and compassionate healers and teachers. I could finally and fully let out my own long-held silent screams and rage since childhood.

This book is written with all the love for hope and healing to all adults who are suffering from childhood neglect, abuse, and trauma. I've written it to increase awareness of this timely, relevant issue from the #metoo campaign to the Turpin children tragedy to the courageous women of the USA gymnastics team. This silent epidemic of harming children is shaping the next generation and leaving a legacy of devastating, lifelong, negative psychosocial effects on adults across the world.

I have a passion to draw public attention back to the stark fact that there is a massive hidden population of emotionally wounded adults across the planet who suffer from post-trauma effects stemming from their upbringing or at the hands of strangers. Many are not veterans of war, but veterans of the war endured in childhood. They are the silent victims, adults, in deep psychological/emotional pain who have difficulty holding jobs, maintaining healthy relationships, self-medicate with prescription drugs and alcohol. They are suffering lifelong, self-tormenting behaviors as survivors of poor parenting, stranger abuse or medical trauma. Unlike veterans, this quietly suffering population is *the* most underserved population I have witnessed in all my years of working with families. They deserve sufficient mental and spiritual resources with expert and compassionate support at an affordable cost. I applaud the few well-respected grassroots foundations such as the National Alliance for the Mentally Ill (NAMI)—where all educational and peer support programs are free of charge—the National Association of Adult Survivors of Childhood Abuse (NAASCA), the National Child Traumatic Stress Network (NCTSN), and the online support group at www.myptsd.com.

As a psychotherapist, I have chosen to break my own silence and come out of hiding to be a voice for the many neglected and abused children across the world. I want to help others understand the psychology behind an entire generation lost to the lonely life of the latchkey era. I want to be a voice for the many survivors who spent most their childhoods bereft of parental care or nurturance and who spent many lonely and terrified nights crying and grieving for any scrap of parental love, comfort or affection.

This is a great time in history for women. Thousands of us are coming forward and standing up against their violators. I also want to stand unashamed with all women across the planet in the #metoo campaign. I am no longer ashamed about what my perpetrators did to me as a defenseless little girl or young woman. Compassionate trauma therapy taught me to place the shame squarely on the violators—where it belongs. In my case, I'm also free because my pain eventually blossomed into full forgiveness *only* through the compassion and forgiveness I finally gave to myself. I wanted to also stand up and use my true, authentic voice for perhaps the first time. Dropping years of social conditioned, ego driven personas, I was able to seek personal self-realization. I wish I had addressed my traumatic childhood years ago and had stopped running. I thought it was better to deal with the devil I knew than the devil I didn't know. That was flawed reasoning. I went to hell and back, but the relatively short twelve-month healing journey freed my soul and my heart and awakened my true divine self.

Finally, I want to offer you hope and all my love, support, and prayers. I hope you will not remain silent about your pain. I hope you honor your body and are gentle on your journey. Please remember that you were a defenseless little child who was trying to make sense of your world, and it was the duty of those adults to protect, nurture, and guide you. If they did not, I am deeply sorry. It is okay to say they failed you miserably as you move toward your own healing journey.

CHAPTER 1

Lonely Latchkey Days

Broken Children

Suzan Gumush

I've come across many neglected children
They carry a pain
That's left a mark
An uncured wound
A broken heart
A broken home
Due to parents disappearing
Or out there searching
Always there children they are hurting
Why! …
Because of greed
Because of need
Because of temptation
Or because of drugs!
These children never did ask to be born
And find their status torn
Ripped apart and shredded!
How selfish can those parents be

All for want and for themselves to repair
The only place they have come to tear
Are the roots of those children
Who live their lives searching for their souls
Life becomes a riddle
When only themselves they muddle
Walking down those empty streets
Meeting up with others who swallowed the same
Now they've decided to create a new game
Let it be violence!
And push those parents into shame
Yet it is always
Those poor children who live with blame!
If this is freedom of choice!
Then let those poor children
Make a voice!

The latchkey generation was a sociocultural phenomenon in America that refers to a specific cohort of children who grew up in the early sixties throughout the early eighties. It also includes children of the greater Westernized world. A latchkey kid or latchkey child returns from school to an empty home because the parent or parents are away at work or a child who is often left at home with little parental supervision. *Latchkey kids* became a common term to describe individuals within Generation X. According to a 2004 marketing study, latchkey children went through their all-important, formative years as one of the least-parented, least-nurtured generations in US history. On September 20, 1982, *People* exposed this profound generation of neglect in an article by Ken Huff entitled: "The Lonely Life of 'Latchkey' Children, Say Two Experts, Is a National Disgrace!"

The latchkey generation is best known for Watergate, the seventies energy crisis, the assassination of Dr. Martin Luther

King, Jr., the first lunar module landing on July 20, 1969, and the first dual-income families and single-parent homes. We were the first generation to *be* latchkey kids and the first generation where one or both parents experienced corporate downsizing and layoffs. We were the MTV and SNL original prime time players generation. The latchkey generation also experienced the highest divorce rates and were the only generation, on average, not to become financially better off than their parents, according to economic statistics.

The latchkey generation also witnessed the landscape of television and music dramatically change during this time to match the new Zeitgeist of the day. Shows were created to represent the new sociocultural phenomena. The days of *Leave It to Beaver* or *Father Knows Best* were being slowly replaced by American and British programming depicting single moms (*One Day at a Time*), single dads (*The Courtship of Eddie's Father*), and working single moms (*Taxi, The Partridge Family*). Britain saw similar media trends with *Days Like These, Bachelor Father, Love Thy Neighbor*. Across England and the United States, the musicians coming of age from the latchkey era also organically conveyed what laid deep within. The lyrics reflected rage, depression, loneliness and suicide ideation. Society experienced the rise of the first heavy metal and grunge bands in the seventies and eighties. The haunting, screaming sounds of Led Zeppelin, Black Sabbath, Pink Floyd, Blue Oyster Cult, and Deep Purple were "characterized by highly amplified distortion, extended guitar solos, emphatic beats, and overall loudness. Heavy metal lyrics and performance styles are sometimes associated with aggression and machismo" according to notations in Wikipedia.

Many latchkey teens found escape in the heart-pounding beats and lyrics. The dark tones gave great comfort to teens who were lost in a world that expressed the rage they felt inside. Teens also turned to the occult and dark fantasy role-playing card games. Dungeons and Dragons debuted in 1974. Teens found avatars that would give them power and voices in a virtual world. Some retreated to seething anger and the desire to hurt others.

Social scientists also refer to the latchkey generation as the first commercial day care generation in order to fill the caregiver vacuum made by primarily mothers entering the workforce for the first time due to financial and sociopolitical reasons. Children were no longer being raised by primary (parents) or secondary (grandparents) familial caregivers that are essential for developing deep family attachments or emotional bonding. Western society had to quickly reorganize and create a new caregiving model, thus we saw the rise of the first childcare mega-industry establishments during the latchkey era. Many mothers who left the home for the workforce during the sixties and seventies had little financial choice however. During the early to mid-1970s, America experienced an energy crisis that left many families to start rationing their household energy by lowering thermostats overnight and being militant about lights being shut off or only being on at certain times of the day. I recall being repeatedly yelled at to shut off my light or not to let the shower or bath water run so long. The gas and energy crisis occurred at the same time the American economy started a downward spiral and the dollar continued to weaken domestic and foreign buying power as well.

On the sociocultural front the feminist movement that began the late fifties and early sixties also grew into an enormous cultural force within the hearts and minds of women. This would spark a spirit of independence and revolution that advocated for all women to gain financial independence, equality, and personal fulfilment by leaving the home (and children) to enter the workplace under the psychosocial mythology they could "have it all" and the children would be just fine. As my mother's generation was coming of age in the early sixties, women fell under this spell and believed, for the first time, they had real choices for financial freedom and equality—a real chance for change. I was four years old in the summer of love in 1967. The summer of psychedelics, and the year the Beatles released *Sergeant Pepper's Lonely Hearts Club Band.* Jefferson Airplane released *Surrealistic Pillow,* and Haight Ashbury was at its apex. Women felt free, liberated, and empowered. They rose up, united, and burned their bras. While these two powerful and unifying socioeconomic and cultural forces were bearing down upon my mother's generation, America's children experienced a maternal exodus, en masse, from homes into the workforce. This produced the rise of the lonely, unparented life of the latchkey and daycare generation.

Women of that era had erroneously been told by pediatric and child-development "experts" of the day that having it all by returning to the workforce did not necessarily equate to negative psychological impacts on their children. They were further led to believe that gender equality and financial independence meant that going to work and coming home, like a man, and resuming parenting duties would leave no lasting psychological ill effects on their children—as long as it was "quality time" the experts purported. Quantity of time spent with a child meeting a child's developing emotional attachment needs not did matter anymore, according to this new mistaken parenting paradigm. And years of research in child developmental psychology was ignored or supplanted.

Did that advice by child experts of the day actually translate to real data generated from longitudinal studies of an entire unparented generation? Or did longitudinal studies and meta-analyses reveal that my generation was truly the generation of childhood interrupted? Was the innocence of children sacrificed upon the altar of parental ignorance? Countless sociological and psychological studies since my mother's generation have been reported in nearly every social and psychological scientific peer-reviewed journal including the *American Psychological Association* on childhood neglect and/or abuse in which history reveals that we were indeed a severely neglected generation due to parental ignorance and the economic necessities of the day. Child psychologists have repeatedly reported their findings for decades in journals and articles. They pinpoint the myriad of lifelong negative emotional and interpersonal consequences that results from failing to meet the emotional and psychological needs just a single child. But no one could have predicted the future tsunami of a generation of adults who now suffer from personal and interpersonal deficits as well as the enormous sociopolitical implications that this unguided generation is experiencing today.

Because neglected children are largely unparented and unguided within the home they rely on strangers for scraps of attention, affection and social learning in their formative years. Neglected children must piece together their worldview from social ques they receive largely from the media and strangers to understand the world around them. This psychosocial patchwork quilt becomes the basis of their constructed reality and worldview, which is shaped by nothing yet shaped by everything. The neglected self is left to wander in the psychological desert, scared and alone. They are unconsciously pushed and pulled this way and that—at the whim of everyone around them—as they constantly seek and scan the emotional climates of others. They have no solid frame of reference to the self. That internal guidance system that should have been established during childhood from a stable, nurturing environment. These survival behaviors are often termed the *orphan syndrome*.

In order for developing children to gain a healthy sense of self or identity they rely on daily nurturance and positive feedback from parents or caregivers that shapes their reality and establishes a worldview of being safe, loved and secure. It comes from modeling adults and gentle guiding social queues at an early age. But when children's reality-building mental skill sets are left to chance in the formative years, their reality is skewed. It becomes a disjointed amalgam of societal conditioning with no internal locus of control. This is when society will pay its highest price when these children come of age, which is what we are experiencing now.

Adult survivors of neglect and abuse often display the behavioral characteristics of a person who has not fully grown up. They are often socially and emotionally immature. They may appear emotionally unstable or perhaps bipolar. Early child neglect and abuse can lead to a discontented mind, unruly and dissonant internal dialogue, or an aggressive drive toward what it wants. Like toddlers, they typically don't care who is in the way. Since they are emotionally stunted they oftentimes throw "adult fits" if they don't get their way within a relationship or workplace. They are psychosocially stuck in the wanting, egocentric stage of child development. Many have arrested development which can result in sociopathy or personality disorders.

According to Leon Festinger's classic theory on cognitive dissonance, the brain—in its primitive state of evolution—does not have the ability to maintain two opposing core beliefs at the same time. Festinger argued that a person will experience profound internal psychological and emotional distress when attempting to reconcile two opposing realities. For many latchkey kids, the loneliness and massive cognitive dissonance between the false media families and their own home lives were too much to bear emotionally. Cognitive dissonance among very young children occurs when they have formed a belief that mommies and daddies love their children and stay together all the time. When divorce, abuse, or neglect occurs at the hands of a parent they love, a distressing emotional dissonance arises and there will be acting out of these negative feelings on some level. A child can only take so much. The psychosocial effects often result in lifelong anxiety, depression, bipolar disorder, or mental illness.

In my practice I often refer parents to Dr. Peter Breggin's outstanding book, *Toxic Psychiatry* that is still relevant today. Dr. Breggin described his book as a "psychiatrist's devastating critique of how the new psychiatry is damaging millions of people, yet biopsychiatry is the dominant ideology of the medical-pharmaceutical establishment."

In his groundbreaking book, psychiatrist Peter Breggin noted that in his thirty years of working with the mentally ill, including children and teens, he was convinced that so-called mental illness behaviors of these children and teens stem from a type of overwhelming "psycho-spiritual break." Breggin further argues that this mind-body disconnect cannot be treated with medication for it was not a result of any so-called chemical imbalance but rather are a result of upbringing and parenting practices in which their emotional and psychological needs were not being met and therefore it would stand to reason they were acting out. He goes on to declare that medication severely impedes the exploration of the psychogenesis of the so-called "illness."

Dr. Breggin has been on the forefront and outspoken opponent against what he terms many of the "school diagnoses." Breggin firmly believes, due to his many decades of experience as a psychiatrist, that any so-called attention deficit disorder (ADD) can ultimately be linked back to what he terms DADD or MADD or "dad attention deficit disorder and mom attention deficit disorder. Indeed many child and developmental psychologists have researched and compared the parenting practices of a punitive, abusive, or neglectful environments with that of a supportive, attentive, and conscious parenting style and compared mentally healthy children and mentally unhealthy children in which the findings still directly correlates with a person's upbringing and environment.

Breggin boldly declared before a several congressional hearings that the natural consequence of the hurried, harried lives of parents, teachers, and siblings leaves little parental time for conscious parenting and loving attention to ground children and give them a settled sense of selfhood, vital for navigating the adult years. These children receive a psychological inheritance of anxiousness (hyperactive central nervous system), insecurity, neuroses, and a whole host of DSM disorders that are ripe to sprout. These seeds of childhood trauma that are sown consciously or unconsciously have resulted in an entire generation of psychosocially stunned individuals seeking "love in all the wrong places" or medicating themselves with pills to get to sleep or at the next cocktail hour. I know—I was there, and I've counselled many that are still there.

Dr. Charles L. Whitfield is an American medical doctor who specializes in assisting survivors of childhood trauma with recovery and associated coping addictions, including alcoholism and prescription drug abuse. He is certified by the American Society of Addiction Medicine, a founding member of the National Association for the Children of Alcoholics, and a member of the American Professional Society on the Abuse of Children. Whitfield has taught at Rutgers University and is a best-selling author. His books about general childhood trauma, childhood sexual abuse, and addiction recovery include *Healing the Child Within* (1987), *Memory and Abuse* (1995), and *The Truth About Mental Illness* (2004).

In an interview about *The Truth About Mental Illness* with psychologist Dr. Jeffery Mislove PhD, Whitfield boldly concluded— after decades in general medicine and psychiatry—that most individuals who suffer from post-traumatic stress disorder are misdiagnosed with depression, anxiety, or personality disorders. In reality, Whitfield states, they are suffering from multiple traumas sustained in childhood. They display similar behavioral presentations, but they are post-trauma stress reaction or complex PTSD (c-PTSD). Whitfield also stated that "by far, the amount of people represented with PTSD and c-PTSD are in the general population and not combat related." This invisible population of hurting, traumatized children become adults. If left untreated, their original trauma bio-programming responses encoded in childhood will continue to express themselves in maladaptive ways and subconsciously drive the behaviors of the individual throughout their lives—regardless of religion, race, socioeconomic status, or education.

As I sit and watch reruns of "That 70's Show" it always solicits a cringe or two as well as laughter. I'm sure many in my generation also see painful reminders in this sitcom of their own upbringing in the authoritarian parenting style of the day. Many hear their own parent's voice in Rhett's sarcastic and aggressive parenting style with his "my way or the highway" house rules or the ever daily threat of "While you are under *my* roof, goddammit, you will follow *my* rules!"

Adults from that era can relate to being reminded, especially during the energy crises, how hard their parent(s) worked to put food on the table, clothes on their backs, and a roof over their heads—as if that was any substitute for a loving, nurturing, and conscious parent. Corporal punishment was rampant as well. If there wasn't a belt, wooden spoon, or stick within grabbing distance of an angry, laid-off, or alcoholic parent, then a good backhand to the mouth—leaving blood and a swollen lip—or a solid punch, especially with young boys, would do. "Backtalk" was forbidden.

For many of the lonely latchkey teens the only form of caring or bonding were at school. We had a few caring teachers or friends and in high school, we felt a sense of empathic camaraderie with the plight of each other for we knew that a majority of us were going home each day, some like myself for their entire school years (K-12) to nothing or no one at the end of the day—day in and day out—until a parent came home to fix dinner and quickly see us off to bed, if we were lucky. Many parents attended night school to improve their chances of getting higher-paying jobs, which naturally extended the amount of time gone and increased their amount of time being unavailable as a parent.

So our generation naturally retreated inward because of the severe isolation and disorienting feelings from child neglect. The television became our babysitter and shaped our worldviews.

As I mentioned, latchkey teens had limited choices for human interaction during those days: school activities, retreating into seventies-style basements with friends to bond together as a makeshift family, getting high, jamming to music, or rocking out with MTV. We tried to numb the messages felt from the single or working parent(s) of neglect, unconscious parenting, or callous snarky remarks as we tried to navigate adolescence without guidance. We were forced to figure life out ourselves, and we became adept at raising ourselves. Teens of the seventies tried hard to manage raging hormones while enduring tired, angry parents yelling about grades, friends, or clothing choices. We were peppered with the ever-present threat of groundings or beatings. This was our life. It is a fact that a child or teen starved for love, emotional attention, and guidance runs the highest risks for the onset of mental illness, chronic physical conditions, and suicide. Some of the highest rates of cancer, alcoholism, and suicide, I believe, come from this generation.

Gripped with paralyzing self-doubt, the latchkey teen's world was built upon profound loneliness from a lack of attention and human interaction from parents or a primary caregiver. Raising ourselves was the foundational upbringing of latchkey kids. By the time high school arrived, we pretty much had this raising ourselves thing down. Our generation were referred to by some as the "mall kids." Groups of lonely kids would find any reason to meet and hang at the mall after school to avoid going home to an empty house again. Tragically, too many of my friends did not want to go home because they might find a laid-off, inebriated parent and confront the evil twin of parental neglect: physical abuse.

More than a few friends had to endure threats and beatings if they broke curfew, attempted to discuss their feelings, dared to speak up for themselves, or let their emotional needs be known. Sadly, the parenting myth of needing to toughen up a child is still with us today and is the leftover legacy of a latchkey worldview.

We have an entire generation still so full of anxiety, depression, and self-hatred as a result. The "my way or the highway" skewed worldview can be seen across an entire generation among the political scene today as a result.

Others, unfortunately, retreated too deeply into their emotional pain and were unable to process the loneliness of neglect. They were tired of being ignored, screamed at, threatened, or hit and decided death would bring them relief as the only alternative. I lost some dear friends to suicide in those days and still grieve the loss of their light in this world. And yet everyone remained in denial. The primary mental health concern among adults and professionals in those days were finding out why teens were so "dark, rebellious and unruly"! No one dared speak of the eight hundred-pound elephant in the room that was the genesis of their behaviors: child neglect and/or abuse. That would have resulted in stigmatizing a parent who was "doing the best they could" rather it was far easier to place the blame on a minor who was struggling through an unparented life. Now a days we just medicate them for compliance.

The loss of friends through suicide was yet another unprocessed and untreated trauma many of us had to endure. Latchkey kids were expected to "buck it up" and carry on. Emotional resilience was demanded among the survivors. Of the survivors I knew of several latchkey teens who became chronically depressed instead of taking their life and received misdiagnoses of oppositional defiant disorder (ODD), Bipolar disorder or clinical depression and with parent's consent went on to fuel the drug industry chemically numbing their brains. They could no longer bear their feelings of being absolutely defenseless against the world from years of non-parental nurturance or guidance and intuitively understood that they were fast becoming adults in a world with no sense of a stable identity, psychosocial skill sets, or meaningful attachments needed to keep them grounded. They had not formed any solid foundational truths about who they were or what their place could be in the world. The latchkey generation did not have the luxury of developing a strong self-esteem when all energies went into surviving each day the best we could. Having little parental guidance the latchkey child constantly scanned the environment for clues about how to behave in order to get basic needs met. Many learned the art of survival more than carefree childhood play. We had to care for ourselves at such a young age and for so many hours each day that a sense of well-being and security was never present. We did not learn to dream like other kids who had parents who were emotionally present. We didn't dare dream about another a life in which parents were emotionally available, greeting us at the door with a smile or a hug. That would just deepened our grief and reinforce our loss.

The literature in child psychology reveals data and reports where children of the latchkey generation became teens and young adults with substantial personal and social deficits in the areas of what term the *golden triangle of psychosocial foundation.* With this foundational model set in childhood, children move confidently into adulthood by building a successful, secure, and happy life. This golden psychosocial triad of emotional health and wellness involves a solid sense of identity that is derived from self-esteem, self-reliance, and—most importantly—self-love. The latchkey child was denied guidance and nurturing in all three psychosocial domains.

Self-esteem, self-reliance, and self-love are the psychological and emotional building blocks and underpinnings for successfully navigating through life's challenges and hardships. When these three emotional states of well-being are solid, a person is resilient and can handle even the most grueling challenges and changes in life with a deep feeling of safety, security, and groundedness. I believe that it is with these three golden keys that unlock the spiritual door as well for all individuals to fully realize, fully individuate, and self-actualize developing into the fullness of their human potential. These are the only keys that matter for a firm psychosocial foundation that allows for growth and development unfettered from limiting beliefs about themselves stemming from a painful childhood. The only keys denied to the latchkey child. Little wonder this generation is listed with so many negative sociocultural firsts among social scientists and child psychologists. It is only years later—through several longitudinal studies and meta-analyses research—that we now have a healthy body of empirical evidence regarding the specific psychosocial deficits among the latchkey generation. What were some of these outcomes listed from a neglected generation whose lack of parenting were deemed "a national disgrace"? Qualitative data from self-reports indicate that this generation, now grown, have some of the lowest self-esteem, sense of self-worth, and self-loving expressions than any other cross-sectional study of society. The results trend more toward a sense of self-loathing, hopelessness, and despair for the future.

I've counseled hundreds in my cohort of the latchkey generation who were brought up to expect to daily return home to an empty house, with no smiles to greet them, no hugs, or a parent interested in how their day ways. They experienced emptiness and loneliness, learning to fend for themselves for after-school nutrition, security, and entertainment after doing homework and chores. Many developed lifelong generalized anxiety disorder (GAD), the nation's top mental health issue. Millions manage their anxiety through alcohol or prescribed benzodiazepines. Many others have co-occurring PTSD that has left many slave to the will of their primitive emotional limbic system when responding to life challenges. They irrationally argue with partners, battle their bosses, and feel overwhelmed about raising their own children. They lack emotional self-regulation.

I've also worked with many people who have fallen into depression. I watch as former classmates of mine are still fighting the demons of yesteryear that arose from the pain of a brutal upbringing, loneliness, and crippling self-doubt. More than a few are still emotionally stuck in the seventies and eighties. They are trying to recapture something that never was or are trying to silence their ghosts with every glass of a wine or whiskey at cocktail hour. Their false, empty laughter hides the great pain of a lost childhood.

The political aggressions and societal polarizations that are taking place in America today where radical violent ideologies are running rampant and social media is filled with cyberbullying and hate speeches from political and corporate leaders, I am convinced that what underlies the dark sociopolitical tone we are experiencing today is a direct result of a generation whose child-rearing practices were charged with being "a national disgrace." Their brutal "my-way-or-the-highway" authoritarianism and abusive parenting practices were documented and exposed, leaving deep psychological trauma and emotional wounds that remain unhealed for the most part. Mean-spiritedness, bullying and hate are permeating American political and the corporate culture like never before. Our generation has succeeded like no other in aggressively shifting the entire geopolitical landscape exhibiting maladaptive behaviors reminiscent of a generational trauma that has not healed its deep psychological wounds.

The violent and aggressive geopolitical climate of today, I believe, is simply reflecting the fears, paranoia, and traumas left over in the psyches of baby boomers, latchkey, and Gen X'ers. It is built upon the traumas from war, postwar scarcity, energy crises, the Cold War, and profound child neglect and abuse leftover from the latchkey era. Voters of these generations view America's future through the lens of their own fear-based childhood environments of tremendous insecurity and trauma. Their worldviews align with the least-nurtured, least-parented, least-guided children in American history. Americans of these generations have psychologically projected their collective and unresolved traumas onto the geopolitical landscape we see today.

Typical trauma behaviors of fear, paranoia, and seeing others as the enemy leads to violence, aggression, and a "let's-get-them-before-they-get-us" mentality of today. Again, these maladaptive ideologies are indicative of post-trauma reactionary responses or a type of collective PTSD. These generations have seen and experienced too much trauma in their lifetime. Sadly, unresolved childhood trauma governs people's behaviors across the life-span and political, religious, and cultural realms are influenced today and could lead to devastating consequences in the future.

CHAPTER 2

Adoption, Early Childhood Trauma, and Epigenetics

Children Learn What They Live

Dorothy Law Nolte

If children live with …
Criticism, they learn to condemn
Hostility, they learn to fight
Ridicule, they learn to be shy
Shame, they learn to feel guilty
Tolerance, they learn to be patient
Encouragement, they learn to have confidence
Praise, they learn to appreciate
Security, they learn to have faith
Approval, they learn to like themselves
Acceptance and Friendship, they learn to find love in the world.

I was conceived in the summer of 1962. My biological parents were not unlike many of today's teenagers who decide to give way to their budding sexuality and hormonally charged urges. Perhaps they were in love—or perhaps it was youthful lust. Either way, their one night of passion would bring forth a baby girl nine months later in April of 1963. When I was born, the young mother was seventeen years old, a junior in high school, and the young man was about to turn eighteen and graduate with hopes of a bright future. Years later, the story was recounted to me. When my biological maternal grandmother found out that her daughter had become pregnant at such a young age and outside of wedlock, she was furious at the thought of her daughter bringing such shame upon herself and the family. She promptly marched her pregnant teen daughter over to the young man's parents' home and demanded accountability and marital resolution. At the time, abortion was illegal and out of the question (hooray for me).

The young man's parents, however, showed little sympathy for the teen girl's plight and placed the blame solely on her. They denied any sentiment of kinship or basic empathy toward their growing first grandchild and sternly announced to both the girl and her mother that they had "plans for their son." Those plans included Annapolis after high school—and did not include being a young father. They were promptly sent packing.

Fueled with a combined rage from social embarrassment, the young girl's mother refused to offer any sympathy or compassion toward her daughter and reminded her of the shame she had brought upon the family. Consequently, she was told that she could not live in her childhood home during her pregnancy because she was a "poor moral influence" on the younger brothers who were still at home. She was to give the baby up for adoption and then come home to resume her education. That scared pregnant teenager packed up her minimal belongings and was taken from the safety and love of her childhood home. She was driven to the local "home for unwed mothers," where she spent the next nine months of her first pregnancy among strangers.

For most women, pregnancy is a time of great joy, happiness, and celebrations. For this young scared teen, pregnancy became her scarlet letter, her shame, her big mistake. I was that mistake.

Over the course of the nine months of my gestation, her own mother refused to call or even visit her. She was completely cut off from any family support, compassion, or love. As was a common parenting practice and social convention for unwed pregnant teens in that day, her mother made the decision to punish her daughter instead of allowing any maternal unconditional love, empathy, or support of her daughter or grandbaby.

My biological mother no doubt had negative and toxic feelings running throughout her body. Feelings perhaps of resentment toward the growing fetus, anger from maternal abandonment, shame, and guilt which science has revealed produces harmful neurochemicals within the body. Naturally, she was frightened. She most likely felt humiliated by the rejection of the father of her child and his family. She likely was traumatized and victimized by the adults around her, and she may have felt resentful about having to be away from her own bed and family home and placed in a strange place among strangers. As I grew and developed in her womb, the formation and cellular foundation of my neurophysiology was built upon this shared mother-baby neurochemical mixture that crosses the blood-brain barrier. It would serve as my biopsychological building block (or template) for life. From the time I was conceived, according to epigenetics, I inherited a neurobiological blueprint of being unwanted and unloved. Scientists are now referring to this epigenetic phenotype as a *gestational generational trauma*.

Years prior to the new science of epigenetics, according to the work conducted by the father of transpersonal psychology, Stanislav Grof, "you are probably more affected by your birth experience than you realize." Grof describes a type of *biological matrix* that contains our emotional imprints and patterns genetically inherited, in part, from mother to child in utero. Grof refers to these as basic perinatal matrices (BPM) and believes that understanding them will open up an entirely new framework for releasing old emotional and behavioral patterns and ushering in personal healing, release of trauma, and achieving higher consciousness.

Fetal development is a beautifully choreographed and symbiotic relationship between two minds and two bodies. Mother and child are one at their very being. Although I was growing and developing biologically on a normal prenatal developmental timeline as a result of my bio-mother's food and vitamin intake nourishing my tiny body in the womb, I received still another neurochemical transmission on a deeper level—in my developing nervous system and cellular memory—at an epigenetic level. My development was governed by genetic changes contained within every toxic feeling that my biological mother felt during the nine months of my gestation.

The psychological feeling states of abandonment, shame, anger, and guilt are believed to be transmitted in utero. Theses *emotional hormones* act as neuromodulators that regulate genetic information and are transferred to the child's developing physical and psychological neuronal matrix. There is some disagreement in the scientific community about the exact neurobiological mechanism of genetic information transfer or even how much negative information is actually transferred to the developing fetus but new research indicates that a large percentage of negative biodata is imprinted from mother to child due to proteins dictating what genes to turn on or off. From a generational trauma perspective, it is understood that, at the subtlest levels of being, neurochemical emotional messages are imprinted onto the child. This is why anxious mothers tend to have anxious children from birth. For me, in many ways, this in utero bio-imprinting was a foreshadowing of my inability to process future childhood traumas. After nine months of fetal development bathed in negative neurochemical messages, my biological markers would compel me to continue to follow the same fear and shame based script of my mother, if you will, on a psychobiological level until I underwent a somatic based holistic, or whole body, treatment for central nervous system response repair and brain rewiring thanks to the brain's neuroplastic properties.

Within an hour of my birth, I was removed by social workers from my biological mother's embrace. She said a brief hello and goodbye to her daughter and I was placed alone in a crib among other newborns who were being put up for adoption. My biological mother recuperated and eventually was allowed to go home again to regain her life and resume high school. Sadly like so many babies however, I did not get to feel the warmth of an excited first-time mother's affectionate smile or get to experience any maternal joy knowing that I had come into this world. My little body never felt the deep emotional, mystical, and spiritual bond between mother and child as I did when my son was born. As a newborn I never felt the warmth of bonding that comes from being nursed and consequently did not receive nature's first immunities, colostrum, that have been found only in mother's milk. Colostrum is a baby's first, strongest, and most organic immunization defending a young infant. Perhaps the reason why I suffered from illness and colic during my early months on this earth. So, I started this life without any of the emotional and physical nourishment that is required for healthy development and spent the next six weeks being taken care of in a home for unwed mothers which was basically and orphanage by any other name.

What we now know in child psychology is that there is a vital period of time in which mother-and-baby bonding provides a primary foundation for learning human social attachment. Child psychologists Mary Ainsworth and John Bowlby showed that this special window of time provides a baby's fundamental sense of safety and well-being. Loving and attentive mother and child bonding time bio-energetically transfers deep feelings of love, acceptance, and security to the baby. Without it, children can develop attachment disorders and deep insecurities. Life outside the womb can be a frightening place with incredible sensory

21

overload for a newborn with bright lights, loud sounds, strange smells, and unknown faces. It is important for young parents to provide maternal and paternal bonding time for attachment and nurturing offering intimacy and connection through mindful presence, tender affection, eye gazing, generous smiles, and joyful cuddling. Sensory overload, or an inability to integrate sensory stimulation, in the absence of parental or caregiver nurturance may result in a *sensory integration deficit disorder*. Childhood trauma can be link to many anxiety based disorders.

I was six weeks old when the adoption agency found a family for me to be placed with. I was placed with a young couple who could not have children of their own and looking back, did not really *want* children. They were following the social conditioning script of getting married, having children and climbing the career ladder. A year prior to my placement my adoptive parents had adopted a baby boy. I was adopted into a middle-class, career and status oriented family. Years later I understood that my older adopted brother had emotional and behavioral special needs from the outset that were far beyond the diagnostic and treatment capabilities of the medical, psychological, and educational systems of the day. And I was to pay the greatest price. Consequently, most of my early childhood trauma and subsequent development of post-traumatic stress resulted from this mixture of odd pre- and post-natal beginnings and family dynamic. To top it off, my growing up years were set within the sociocultural context and backdrop of the neglectful latchkey era.

Even during my pre-school days, I sensed that my mother resented being a stay-at-home mom until I entered kindergarten. She was miserable handling two small children, changing diapers, feedings and handling domestic duties. Even as a toddler I could feel she was unhappy being at home all day and taking care of my brother and me. She had already suspended her career for the first four years of my life and couldn't wait to get back to the workforce. My mother was a strong survivor and had been a highly successful woman even prior to marrying my adoptive father. She had survived scarlet fever being bed bound for her entire seventh grade and had gone on to put herself through business college earning what is equivalent today to a bachelor's degree in business. She had successfully begun to build a career prior her marriage and adopting two children. Until the day she died, it was evident that she had always derived her self-esteem and self-worth from the workplace. She felt stuck at home during this period. She had no relatives in town to help with child-rearing.

It was during this period that my developmental trauma episodes began. It started off as little things where I would somehow—just being a kid—annoy my mother. She would get fed up and rage out! On several occasions, which seemed to go on for years, my mother would aggressively brush back my hair always insisting that my long hair be pulled back into a neat ponytail. She demanded we always looked our best in the event a neighbor might pop over. It was during these unpleasant episode that she'd perceive a back talk and she'd haul off and slap me repeatedly in the face with the comb.

I used to stand there in utter shock, unable to run, as she had me by the hair, or retaliate in any way. My little cheeks would swell up and began to sting turning bright red, leaving swollen marks from the comb's teeth. There were many instances when my face would be violently hit without warning when she perceived "lip" or backtalk. By the time I reached my preteen years she no longer used a comb when she could just backhand me across the mouth leaving a bloody, swollen lip. I still have a tendency to flinch when there are sudden movements around my face due to childhood trauma conditioning because there is psychological information always stored in the body termed as body memory.

My mother's annoyance at being a stay at home mom increased and so did the violence against me. When I was around four years old, my brother complained to our mother that I refused to play tag with him. Furious at my "stubborn nature" she grabbed a wooden spoon and came after me. By that time I had gotten used to her lunging at me so I ran toward my bedroom—as if that offers any protection of a child against an angry adult. On this particular occasion she grabbed my little arm, jerked me out of my bed, and asked why I had to be so difficult and not play with my brother. She proceeded to slap my tiny legs repeatedly with the wooden spoon and she demanded I play tag with my brother. As I wailed at the assault on my little body my screams fell on deaf ears. She proceeded to drag me by my long hair down the hallway to play this dysfunctional tag game with my brother. I cried and cried, wanting her to let me go but she continued to hit me until I "tagged" my brother.

This domestic violence episode began to model to my brother that it was ok to be abusive to me, for children indeed learn what they live just as the poem of the start of this chapter refers. During this terrifying episode my brother laughed and laughed as he ran down the hall so he could be tagged. Though I loved my family, my mother and brother horrified me, and I was left stunned at their cruelty. This would not be the last or the worst of it for me.

For the next decade, I had to silently endure my brother's cruelty and violence and my mother's neglect and disdain for me. Both left deep psychological and spiritual wounds that would severely impact my personal, interpersonal, and professional relationships for the next five decades. I felt alone and trapped in that dysfunctional home. I loved my family, but I could not understand why they did such things to me or why my mother did not love me. A child does not have the advanced cognitions online to realize these behaviors are more of a reflection of the perpetrator than the innocent child. So they internalize such maltreatment and begin to second guess themselves. It is important to realize that thoughtless or cruel acts parents inflict on their little ones out frustration or anger have been shown to cause a lifetime of psychological scarring and oftentimes there remains terror in the child even when the parents think the child will not remember due to their small age but in truth is still stored at the cellular level in the form of traumatic body memory.

In addition to my early years of child maltreatment and latter parental neglect by my adoptive mother, prior to my parent's divorce, I also experienced a few traumatic experiences with my adoptive father. I don't recall spending much time with my dad in my early years because he worked a lot, but I do remember recall a few traumatic incidents he caused.

This kind of trauma left in my body however, was of a different flavor than child abuse/neglect. This takes the form of when parents think they are "being funny" or getting a laugh at the expense of their child or just plain thoughtlessness, not thinking of how a young child might perceive the situation or their actions. For example, I used to watch *America's Funniest Videos* years ago where many of the stunts, accidents and foibles are truly hysterical. But once in while there would be a child being terrified at the expense of the parent which was difficult to watch. One such dad, as I recall, decided to play a "joke" on his daughter who was around six or seven years old. As his young daughter sat in the back of his convertible, Dad decided to start screaming at her "oh no! It's going to eat you!" as the roof was coming up back in place. The sheer terror in her poor eyes and blood curdling screams that came from her as she yelled, "no! Don't let it get me!" Young children rely on their parents to protect not torment so for me, those clips were hard to sit through. Of course dad was oblivious and laughing all the while at her expense.

So on a few occasions my own dad thoughtlessly, without malice, subjected me to similar events causing central nervous system overwhelm that stayed with me for decades to follow. One such incident occurred when I was around six years old. My dad was holding me on a family outing touring the then, Olympia Brewing Company in Olympia, WA. Being so young, I did not understand or care about the beer-brewing process but I was fascinated by the vast expanse of the brewery, the rich smell of the hops, and the shiny brass vats that stirred the hop mixtures. The vats were enormous, and the liquid brew was meticulously cooked, stirred, and washed by these large blades that were approximately twenty feet long. They continuously went around and around, stirring the hops mixtures throughout the day. On the second there was a small door opening to these vats where visitors could peek into them and watch the huge blades slowly going around. I don't really know if he thought he was being funny or he thought I wanted a closer look, but all of a sudden, my dad put me fully inside the opening. Immediately the sheer terror looking down sent a bolt of electricity throughout my body. I was in fight-or-flight mode and had a full trauma response.

I began screaming, like the previous child I mentioned, hysterical with fear. The huge blades were swirling, and I saw nothing but the inside of the enormous vat until he decided to pull me out. My heart was pounding. My central nervous system was sending lightning bolts of shocks throughout my body and my brain went into shut down or freeze mode. My primitive brain and body signals were letting me know that this was potentially a life-threatening event.

Years later, again I recalled an event in which my body would simultaneously feel terror along with the pain of feeling electrocuted or having electricity running throughout my central nervous system. That event was immensely traumatic for me in which small spaces and a fear of being trapped in fast cars were a trigger for me. It may surprise readers to learn that my dad was in law enforcement, a state patrolman. On one rare occasion my dad took me to the state patrol office with him where frankly I was happy to be away from my mother and brother. Besides I was very proud of my dad and wanted to know him more. He worked all the time, it seemed, during my younger years and prior to my parent's divorce. So this was a treat. Or so I thought. While dad briefly spoke to his supervisor, I was instructed to sit down and wait for him in the lobby. As I sat there I glanced at several black-and-white photos on the walls that depicted the consequences of drunk driving from a public service announcement campaign the state patrol was running. My emotions were horrified by the many pictures that were inappropriate for children. For years I suffered from nightmares recalling one picture in particular that showed a drunk driver's severed head approximately twenty feet from his smashed vehicle and remaining body.

The last traumatic incident involving my dad prior to divorcing my mom was when I was sitting in the back seat of his car when another motorist cut him off. My dad was off duty and we were in his personal car. It became evident that he completely disregarded the fact that his young daughter was in the back seat and proceeded to floor it, using his highly trained law enforcement vehicular skills and terrifying me. While dad was furiously chasing the offending vehicle he was weaving in and out of traffic. Needless to say, I was left wide-eyed and white with fright. Once again this thoughtless parental act left my child's body in a perceived life-threatening state of terror and trauma. I had been exposed to his careless parental action again being unfairly trapped with an inability to run from the terror.

I cannot emphasize enough that parents must remain diligent and parent consciously. Things parents believe are funny are often not funny to children. They can be frightening. It is important to understand that young children do not have the cognitive ability to process shock or excruciating fright. The trauma literally sent electric shock waves of tingling throughout my body.

Like many in the latchkey era, my parents divorced when I was nine years old and I was stigmatized as being from "broken home." As a therapist I've counselled hundreds of divorcing parents, educating them on the negative and long lasting effects that divorce has on children. I've provided support and several resources available to help children and teens cope with their parent's divorce and the negative effects. I get asked many times if there is a right age or right way to divorce. I can tell you there is no right age as each child will be negatively affected to some degree and will also internalize their parent's splitting up as somehow their fault. As do doing it right, research in child psychology and development shows the healthiest way to mitigate the negative effects is to tell the children together as you remind them divorce is an adult issue and has nothing to do with the, all the while reassuring both parents are committed to their upbringing and assurances of unconditional love. Afterwards, there needs to be consistency and never using the child as a go between or speaking badly of the other parent. Likewise, so many teen boys tend to be used by grieving or depressed mothers as surrogate spouses which is psychologically detrimental to the teen and not his responsibility to fill that role when trying to navigate the uncertain years of adolescents himself.

After my parents separated, my mother fell into a type of depression known as dysthymia (chronic low-grade depression). It drove her to work longer and longer hours where my brother and I experienced increased parental neglect. My brother and I, like so many latchkey kids, would be left at home without parental supervision for long periods of time both before and after school as well as, in my case of a single mother, sometimes as late as seven o'clock at night. This lack of parental supervision due to economic reasons left space for mischief and with my situation, increasing cruelty inflicted on me by my brother. He was unsupervised and unruly. His special needs with his lack of self-control was to become more evident and I was to pay a high price for a parent who wasn't around much during those lonely latchkey years. I was trapped once again by the circumstances that adults had put me in.

It began early in my elementary years where I would come home alone with no parent. Little things at the beginning where my brother would come up to me and just haul off and knock me down when I returned home from school. Being two years older, he was naturally bigger than me. When he felt like it he could easily pin me down and hold me down for long periods laughing and spitting in my face or pulling my hair out at its roots. I would wrestle and struggle and fight until my body was exhausted as he sat on me laughing. Oftentimes throughout the years I would finally give up, exhausted and crying while struggling to breathe under the weight of his body. He would often threaten me of it getting worse if I told anyone. This is how family domestic violence is often concealed. Threats of getting worse are the seeds of toxic secrecy that leave children prisoners in their own homes. It was like a dirty family secret held within my terrified and traumatized body. I remained a silent victim of parental neglect and horrific sibling and stranger abuses for a total of eleven years. This life of neglect and abuse is all I knew growing up.

Unlike children who are raised with loving, supportive and attentive parents, my home was never a place of security, love or safety. So as with most children of developmental trauma, I became adept at stealth and surveillance in my own home. It was surviving the battlefield of childhood and I was fast developing post-traumatic stress disorder unbeknownst to me. Most of my cognitive energies focused on cultivating that skill. I had little time for playing or indulging in creativity or imagination—the vital ingredients for healthy psychosocial development. I learned to avoid being in the vicinity of my brother after school at all costs, and I most definitely avoided coming within striking distance.

I did find a sanctuary in those early elementary school days were we had a large wooded area at the edge of our housing development. Many times after school I would bolt out of the house and run away from him when his anger got really out of control. I learned to become a survivalist in elementary school. I learned to climb trees quickly and quietly, build secret places in the woods, and hide. I even dug a hole and built a kind of bunker from downed limbs where I could quickly lay down in the dirt covering myself with the huge limbs for concealment listening for his footsteps, praying he wouldn't find me to begin his many tortures on my body.

If I was unfortunate and happened to be "caught" by him after school, many times he'd also grab me and tie me to a chair and leave me in my dark room for several hours. As I screamed and pleaded, I could hear him laughing outside the door the entire time. If the fancy struck him, I would also find myself being dragged by my hair down the hall, reminiscent of the early preschool days when mother modeled this behavior to my brother during the dysfunctional tag game. If I really made him angry by standing up for myself things got exponentially worse for me. He would "slug" or pinch me really hard leaving nasty bruises. And if I didn't move out of his way fast enough, he would slap my head or knock me down. These were weekly occurrences that lasted years. My brother was also cruel to animals. It started with burning ants on the sidewalk and quickly progressed to placing a string of fireworks down a rain boot with an opossum in it and lighting it on fire! He would grab my neck and force me to look at his cruel, bloody handiwork. As we aged, his cruelty also turned on the family dogs. He would poke them with sticks and tease them to madness.

Any assault on a child's body—slapping, pinching, pulling hair, and spanking—causes trauma and arrests the normal psychosocial development of the brain and central nervous system. At the time of this writing, I was so pleased to read that France has voted to enact the "Equality and Citizenship" bill, which places a countrywide ban on all forms of corporal punishment, including spanking. It was created to eradicate all forms of "degrading, cruel, and humiliating" treatment of kids by their parents" (*USA Today*, 2017).

I tried desperately to lay low, play it small, be invisible, and stay out of everyone's way. A theme that would become how I went through my life. It wouldn't be until decades later that I would learn to overcome my belief that I did not have a right to my opinion let alone could express my voice in this world. I had to process my trauma to fully live who I was instead of playing small or invisible. I knew I had much more to give in life, but I was terrified of "being seen" by anyone since that always meant being noticed and struck down. I would end up shrinking inside as every part of my personhood would become chronically violated over the years, and I learned that my home and my body were not safe places.

Not surprisingly I also developed a phobia of tight spaces in adulthood that derived from the many times my brother also forcefully put me into my small clothes drawers. I could hardly breathe or move while he would block the drawers with his legs and hands, again laughing until I was hysterical with terror. I endured that living coffin many times. Another "game" he would play was to hide under my bed and wait for me quietly. When I would sit down on my bed, he would grab my ankles and laugh while I tried to kick him loose. When I did manage to break free, I would run to the safety of Mother Nature once more and hide in the woods. If it was an unlucky day where I could not break free, he would jerk me so hard to the floor. I literally had no footing under me. Once again, my cries would be minimized or excused as excessive tattling or exaggerating. After all, don't all siblings get into it? All my bruises were considered normal consequences of childhood sibling play. At times, I would express outrage at this injustice. I would plead with my mother for any kind of protection, but my brother would only receive a mild verbal scolding and a warning to leave me alone or be grounded. Neither ever occurred. The warmer weather was always my salvation. I stayed in the woods or with friends under the watchful eye of neighbors for any kind of protection.

During my elementary school days I began to experience physical and—for the first time—sexual abuse by adults *outside* of the home as well as the lack of parental supervision and sibling terror in the home. Most children enter first grade with a little trepidation mixed with a whole lot of excitement backed by supportive parents who encourage them on the journey of growth and independence. I entered a classroom with a teacher who used abusive and uneducated methods against a left-handed child and would daily strike my knuckles with a ruler when I was learning to write. Just when I thought public school would offer me a safe place from the tortures at home I was again to be disappointed by adults.

It is still difficult for me to fathom that such an ignorant and egregious mind-set against left handed children was still pervasive in the early sixties among some educators. But my teacher insisted that I learn to write with my right hand. No matter the abuse, pain, humiliation, or embarrassment she caused me, I was clearly— and most definitely would remain—left-handed. This incident was added to the list in a long line of developmental traumas I would come to experience. The violence and horrible physical abuse on my little hand went on until the teacher informed my mother that I was "handicapped." She further declared that she was "working" with me. My mother, thankfully, took offense and promptly reported the teacher. The principal put a stop to the blatant abusive practice.

Another incident outside the home occurred when later around seven years old, I was invited to go roller-skating for my friend's birthday party. My friend's mother came to pick me up, and I was excited to get out, meet new friends, skate, and have fun. When I approached the counter to get my skates, the man behind the counter asked my skate size. He also offered to help tie them for me. Before I realized what was happening, he grabbed me, placed me directly in front of him with the public behind us, and began tying my skates. I remember being uncomfortable because the shag carpeting on the counter was scratchy on my little legs. I had worn modest little-girl shorts, but had a mounting feeling of uneasiness with that employee. No one approached the counter to ask for skates for some time. Before I knew what was happening, that man put his hands up my little shorts and molested me in broad daylight. I pushed his hand away vigorously, jumped down, and ran to tell my friend's mother.

Because this sexual violation was not contained inside our home and at that time my parents were not yet divorce it could not be ignored by my parents. When my dad found out, the man was arrested, arraigned, and sentenced for child sexual assault. Adding trauma to trauma however, again insensitive and thoughtless adults had forced me to *show* male adult detectives "where he touched you" within forty-eight hours of the violation. I was pressured by adults to disclose and reenact the disgusting event at seven years of age. Once again I was flooded with humiliation, feelings of a lack of adult protection, betrayal by my parents, and my heart felt physically hurt and broken beyond repair. It was an outrageously insensitive request by adults and law enforcement from a child who had just been violated in such a way, but was also typical of how the system fails children time and time again by not considering the psychological or emotional damage a reenactment might cause. I dare say that no one needs a degree in psychology to understand that the seeds of victimhood and post-trauma effects would begin to develop and bloom into full fruition as I began to resign myself early on to the fact that my life would entail neglect, abuse and no protection as I imagined I would continually attract unkind, unloving, and perverted people of all ages. That humiliating experience was just one more nightmare stacking upon the last; the thematic neglect/abuse story of my short life was being played out over and over again. Each was as traumatizing as the last.

As a young girl I learned helplessness and how to disassociate from my body. I hid all my shame, my torment, my pain, and my broken heart and spirit from everyone for my entire life—until now. Even as a young child though, I would promise myself not to fall into utter despair despite being unwanted and unloved, abused and traumatized for the first decade of my life on this earth. For the next ten years, I comforted myself with the knowledge that someone I would be grown and free. I willed myself to be happy and smile on the outside. I became an expert at hiding my shame and pain. My mind started to develop a dark worldview however. I began to internalize a belief that neglect and abuse were my lot in life. In my body, the seeds of terror had fully bloomed into systemic fear of the world and everyone in it. I realized quickly the stakes were higher for those who preyed on little girls.

I cried so many nights not wanting to believe I had really been rejected by two sets of parents and now was being abused by my only other family member, my brother. Aren't parents supposed to love and protect their children? Aren't brother supposed to love and protect their sisters? My life was a nightmare with all the cognitive dissonance my reality contained. Many nights, I thought, does no one care? There must not be a loving god. I cried over the realization that I had been placed in a family where the mother put her career before her children's needs. Where she was caught up in her own life that she did not care to protect me. And I was in a hopeless situation with a special needs' brother who had serious behavioral problems. Additionally, I was assaulted by my first grade teacher and told I was handicapped because I was born left-handed. I was further sexually molested by a stranger at the skating rink. It was more than any child should bear in the first years of life.

As I grew, my mother also began to verbally abuse me and often called "a snot-faced liar." One of her hard to understand threats included threatening to "knock my head into a peak and knock the peak off," which I always thought was a funny way of threatening physical violence as I tried to imagine such a thing. I wanted to chuckle every time I heard that phrase, but I did not dare risk another slap across the face as I had too many of those growing up.

As one can imagine growing up in an environment such as this I had no sense of security, wellness, or self-identity. I was out of touch and disassociated from my body. I had no real understanding of what an appropriate, loving, and nurturing family was and I struggled emotionally and psychologically for decades as I tried to make sense of my early years of childhood.

Abuse and neglect were the very reasons I entered the study of psychology as a scientific discipline. I wanted to study the minds of individuals who would do such a thing to their child or another person's child. I made it my life's mission to find out the motive behind such cruel and outrageous behaviors. I also wanted to find a way to relieve my own symptomology of profound fears. I struggled with panic attacks, phobias, and disassociation, all of which are the protective mechanisms of the psyche that will not allow an individual to utter collapse. It is little wonder that victims tend to develop attachment disorders, generalized anxiety disorders, or complex PTSD after growing up in such environments. I knew I would end up fighting every day of my life *not* to believe the evidence all around me, that I was a little girl who no one saw, heard, loved, or even cared for. I often lost that battle, and the trauma and fatigue left me in mental shambles.

A young and innocent child's heart and mind cannot comprehend a parent who does not love them. The child of neglect and abuse emotionally and physically starves for the vital life-nurturing forces that are necessary for healthy child development. Forming healthy attachments to others provides a child with a sense of positive self-worth, a healthy identity, security, and a sense of safety. When a child is violated or unloved, this sense of safety and security is violently ruptured. The child starts to develop a sense of insecurity, a disassociated sense of self, and a worldview that everyone is to be feared and not trusted.

It is a basic parental responsibility to provide a child with love, nurturance, and emotional grounding for a child's healthy sense of self to develop into a loving adult. When parents are unhealthy, they have their own emotional/psychological deficits that are passed along generationally to their children. And when parents do not meet the emotional needs of their children, they too develop *developmental deficits* thus are *deficient* in emotional security, love, and stability. Children of neglect, abuse, and other traumas come of age with many psychosocial deficits that prevent them from venturing into the world knowing how to protect themselves.

As adults, they are often emotionally stunted and psychosocially stuck. They subconsciously enter relationships seeking mother figures or father figures and end up with partners who are much older than they are. They have unmet emotional needs for motherly or fatherly nurturing. Many adult survivors of childhood trauma have codependent behaviors as well, are emotionally needy, and display emotional dysregulation as adults. The inner child often acts negatively toward a partner, a boss, or a friend. These behaviors are indicative of an inability to fully develop healthy emotional regulation. This dysregulation stems from developmental traumas or not getting their emotional needs met as a child.

After the incident at the skating rink and my parent's divorce, my mother moved my brother and me to a new city. We were given our first set of house keys at the start of fifth grade. We had been officially initiated as latchkey kids and were instructed not to bother our mom at work unless it was an absolute emergency. We were not to call even to report that we arrived home safely, let alone for her to ask how our day had been. Her behaviors reinforced that she didn't care, but sadly I was used to the maltreatment after so many years.

I had developed some new friendships in this new town. Many of whom also had their own house keys dangling around their necks or in their pockets. Funny thing is, we felt grown up in an odd sort of way. In our preteen minds, we imagined ourselves being viewed as responsible adults. After all, weren't we responsible? Wasn't it a fact that for years many of us had gotten ourselves up, dressed, either had a hot breakfast meal provided by the school or poured ourselves cold cereal and saw ourselves out the door walking to school alone or meeting up with a friend along the way together? Likewise, I would walk home alone, using my house-key to get in and if I was lucky enough to avoid my brother I would get some after-school nutrition, do my homework, and do the chores by the time Mom returned home sometime in the evening. I had done this routine in the formative years of growing up since entering the first grade so by the fifth grade I pretty much could take care of myself. Day after day and year after year for twelve years it was the same lonely latchkey routine. The tortures I received at home from my brother continued daily with horrific after school fights. And as grew my body began to fully manifest post-traumatic responses for the first time from years of domestic abuse and my mother minimizing and rationalizing these attacks. Little did I know, the worst was yet come still.

When I was in sixth grade I was walking to elementary school alone as I had done nearly every morning for six years. While standing on the corner of a busy arterial waiting to cross over to the school campus, an old pickup truck drove up and stopped at the stop sign beside me. I glanced quickly to see if he was going to turn or let me cross. All of a sudden, the driver leaned his large body straight up in the seat, and fully exposed himself to me while yelling, "Hey, little girl, how do you like this?"

That was my first real PTSD episode in which my body completely reacted and took over and my reasoning ability shut down or went "offline." Like the many other incidents early in my life, I was in full terror and panic mode. But this time when my fight-or-flight response took over my body had an escape and that was right into traffic. Before I could even think, my body had bolted across the busy street—without looking for oncoming cars! The years of developmental trauma had built up or rather developed in my body which now had unconsciously propelled me away from the threat and toward safety. As my heart was pounding, I ran toward the school. I heard him turn and speed away.

With the advances in technology neuroimaging of the PTSD brain has supported this notion that a trauma response does blocks higher order reasoning abilities in the frontal lobe regions of the brain and when a person is terrified, the seat of our emotions called the limbic system is lit up with activation, the more primitive regions of the brain. Therefore a PTSD "attack" will trigger neural firing of the emotional centers of the brain and activate the motor neurons to quickly move the body away from perceived danger in the absence of any kind of self-regulation of the executive functioning centers or logical brain. Recall that "neurons that fire together, wire together" so given enough fight or flight responses continually in childhood is therefore the foundation for emotional *dysregulation* and bodily *disassociation* that lasts a lifetime until repaired. These are simply classical conditioning (stimulus/response) behaviors.

So as I grew my body and mind were in a chronic dissociative state where my body was essentially hijacked when a post-trauma response would present, oftentimes I could not control it, as I mentioned, due to classical conditioning causing emotional dysregulation from multiple developmental traumas. Put another say, with any perceived threat in which the limbic system begins rapid firing there is a shut-down of any rational thought in the frontal lobes—a hallmark symptomology of a trauma response. When individuals appear too emotional or illogical in any given situation it is vital we have compassion first and perhaps consider there may be roots of past unhealed traumas in their life.

Terror, threats, and torture were an ever present reality for many growing up without parental supervision during the latchkey years. And like many of my friends, it was a family secret that we did not dare tell any adults about our experiences. Deep down many of us knew foster care would be worse. Years of childhood neglect and abuse had classically conditioned me that involving adults to protect me would probably bring about more humiliation and embarrassment and possible removal from the home. After all, weren't we supposed to grow up and buck it up in the seventies?

Not surprisingly, I was becoming hardened in the heart. I'd had so much of my innocence stolen, and so I started acting out like so many kids do with a trauma history. So in sixth grade, I got in trouble with school authorities for the first time. I was at that age of discovery of the opposite sex, had spent a majority of my young life raising myself and looking after myself. Our curfew was when the street lights came on. We ran the streets in the 70's and I had developed street smarts-- the seeds of rebellion.

My first boyfriend was in the sixth grade. He was a latchkey kid also who, one day, had smuggled a pint of vodka onto the elementary school grounds. We were walking across the school grounds when another student saw the bottle sticking out of his back pocket and reported us. We hadn't consumed any yet, and I think he was trying to act "like an adult" as he had witnessed at home. He was suspended from school for three days and left alone at home, which made his neglect and emotional state worse. I was grounded for two days and told not to consider him my boyfriend any longer. Neither adult punishment made any difference to either of us as we knew they were just doing what parents do, punishment without parental teaching or even caring to find out the root cause of the behaviors—parental neglect. History in parenting practices have revealed that children lacking thoughtful, loving parents end up rebellious, wild and unruly. And to the extreme there are cases in which neglected children are so developmentally delayed they are mute and even feral from the lack of love and nurturing from responsible adults in their lives. Many of us ran the streets until ten o'clock at night even in fifth grade and thought nothing of it. Some pre-teens would consider this lifestyle freedom but much to the contrary those days and nights were extremely lonely for the latchkey children of the seventies.

The following year in seventh grade where teen angst and

hormonal fluctuation are at their height and self-esteem is at its lowest, I was started to really manifest complex PTSD symptomology even in the absence of any trigger. This was the beginning of my frequent night terrors with flashbacks where I'd wake up screaming and soaked in sweat. I would have daily emotional outbursts full of anger at my mom, my brother, my teachers and the world in general. I started to really develop internal hate derived from a cumulative effect of parental neglect and my mother's unwillingness to protect me from my brother or strangers over the years or even take me seriously. So I began experimenting with cannabis and used as often as I could get some just to calm my brain and body down. I had suffered for so long and had the hands of so many that I had had enough. In addition, due to years of verbal assaults from my mother calling me a "snot-faced liar," a "little shit," and a "whore" it had severely eroded any semblance of self-worth I had begun to develop over my short years on this earth. I suffered from extreme low self-esteem and had zero confidence in myself, but I was determined to get free someday and "become someone" despite my ugly upbringing.

During the latchkey era, middle schools began to offer life skills classes embedded into the school course offerings. This was in response to the overwhelming amount of single family homes and mothers who had entered the workforce leaving little time to teach their children essential life skills. Whereas parents of previous generations had the time to teach their children how to cook, sew, type, make a budget, or even balance a checkbook, middle schools saw courses offered in home economics, typing, auto shop, and woodworking. For many, these classes became our only means of gaining essential life skills as we entered high school. Domestic and life skills training were placed squarely on the school system, and where I learned most of my practical skills for life, not from my mother.

Over the next few years I would get brief respites of relief from my brother's after-school tortures by becoming involved in several after-school sports and activities: varsity tennis, gymnastics, campfire girls, varsity cheerleading, and the swim team. In the summer, my mother would put me in a residential campfire camp where I was relieved to be out of the home for an extended period of time. Participation in after school sports and activities allowed my body a brief respite from the onslaught of verbal and physical abuse and the strenuous activities also provided my nervous system an outlet for my body's stored trauma. These activities and camps were my salvation in the middle school years. The tumultuous life of the middle school years however would bring a new kind of trauma in my life for the first time—the school bully.

One day while I was walking to class, I felt a slam against my shoulder and my back was forced up against the lockers. A crowd of students started to gather until it felt like nearly half of the seventh grade stopped and was staring at me. A female bully zeroed in on me, her target, with a sardonic smile and gritted teeth. She and her buddy were a grade higher and had eyed me as an easy target coming into seventh grade. Not having any parental guidance over my formative years I was still naive in so many ways. Bullies can sense an air of vulnerability in others, and I had seem to have a target on my back all my life. I figured it was just another episode I was going to have to deal with and would buck up after it ran its course. She had verbally threatened to beat me up before, which caused me to run home the minute the bell rang quite a few times. This time, she was brazen enough to attack me during the school day and was standing in front me, ready to do real business.

All of a sudden as if reliving years with mother and my brother, I received a full-swing, open-handed slap across my face in full view of that juvenile audience. Although shocked, I paid little attention to my already dissociated body having been slapped so many times in my life. My only concern was as I watched my three-ringed binder and textbook fly toward the ground I said a quick prayer that the binder would not land on its apex, causing the dreaded pop that would send all my papers flying—but of course it did exactly that. Humiliated, I did not even look up as the students dispersed at the bell. I simply picked up my textbook and papers and as so many times before, told no one. Neither did anyone else. That meant involving adults, and I knew that wouldn't go well for me.

I struggled to think of what this girl had against me or how I became her unfortunate victim, but she and her sidekick were the known female bullies in the middle school. I was used to this treatment and naturally blamed myself but as we all now know, the problem with the bully, not the victim. Bullies are typically insecure and lack self-love typically stemming from a lack of love in their homes, so they act out and will usually pick on anyone just to vent their hate, making them feel more in control, since their lives are typically out of control. These two girls were simply products of their upbringing. They had single working mothers and were forced to raise themselves during the latchkey days as well. Some handled it better than others. These two would run the streets and school looking for vulnerable kids to pick on to somehow ease their own pain and abate their own anger, making themselves feel powerful in their own powerless, unhappy lives. These bullies were eventually expelled after causing so much trouble with students and teachers.

I received a miracle however, an answer to years of personal prayer (we were not a religious family) when I was in the seventh grade. My mother would re-marry, and a loving, supportive stepdad entered my life. The only real "parent" I would ever know. I always felt sorry for my stepdad (just Dad now). He entered his first marriage without full disclosure of the history of my mother, brother, and me. He was solid working man from Indiana who was raised by a loving family on the farm. He was one of five children and worked hard on the farm beside his father and brothers while his mother stayed at home to raise the kids and cook all the meals. And here he was about to take on a dysfunctional trio of epic proportions, where he was to become more than a little despondent and bewildered about how to both love and handle all of us.

At the time, all I wanted was a lock on my bedroom door. I decided to approach my new stepfather about my brother's harassments without disclosing the embarrassing horrors of my childhood. I pleaded with him for a lock to my bedroom. And although he had no idea why Dad was sympathetic to my pleadings so for the first time in my life an adult actually did something to protect me. Although I did not know what love felt like, I was happy he took me seriously and that was enough for me. So being the carpenter he was he installed a lock on my bedroom door. For the first time in my life I felt safe. That was to be a shattered illusion and I would never again feel safe in my life until I entered my trauma therapy.

Years later after having raised my own family I sat down with dad and confessed all of the horrors that occurred to me before he entered my life. He told me that he did wonder why I was so hysterical many times and thought I was just an over-reactive pre-teen experiencing hormones. He admitted he had no idea! He said, "I just thought, *Doesn't every brother bother his sister?*" He did not know the depths of abuse or emotional damage that was caused by the lack of parental nurturing or protection I endured as a toddler and young girl. And having experienced so much at a young age, with threats to keep the family secrets, I wasn't about to tell this new person in my life the extent to which my brother had attacked me, molested me, or tortured me since as far back as I could recall.

When my step-dad came into our lives my brother was nearly fourteen years old. He seemed to get angrier, especially since there *might* be a new person to protect me. He had gotten used to eleven plus years of doing what he wanted to his little sister and wasn't about to stop. Since he was a young boy he struggled with untreated special needs, dyslexia and challenges with emotional regulation. The years of parental neglect and no male father figure took its toll on him as well. When my dad entered the picture he was struggling with increased anger and emotional dysregulation that comes with the onset of testosterone so our fights became more violent as we both got bigger and stronger. I spent the remainder of my middle school years and most of high school years after school locked in room my room, at a friend's house, or at the mall when I had no after school activities.

I was to experience two more horrific traumas however before my middle school days were over. Believe it or not, these events were even worse than the first eleven years of my life and left such deep emotional scarring and trauma imprints in my body and mind.

When I entered eighth grade, I befriended a very shy and lovely girl who kept to herself because everyone thought she was "weird." I had other friends from sports and campfire girls but was drawn to this sweet quiet sensitive soul who seemed to be so mercilessly marginalized. We became kindred spirits and good friends. When I found out her home was on the way to my house, we would often walk together after school until we had to walk down different streets. She had the sweetest smile, and her eyes would light up when she laughed. She was a true friend, and my heart was not scared to take a chance to believe there were authentic, kind people in the world.

Our brief friendship was cut too short and my heart was to be shattered a thousand times over as I dove back into rebellious c-PTSD darkness. We were in class when we heard an announcement for an unscheduled all-school convocation in the gym. As the students settled down, we listened to a very somber message from the principal. The gymnasium was flanked by teachers and the school counselor as we waited with concern and anticipation. The principal, with bowed head, notified the student body he had very sad news. That lovely, shy, beautiful young soul was struck by a car in the crosswalk the day prior—the day I had an after-school sport—and was killed.

My world was shattered. I was sick, faint, and speechless. I had few friends I could confide in, and now she was gone. It wasn't fair! I hated life, my school, my family, everyone! I wished I could be with her to forget all my pain. I was numb and dizzy. I was dissociated. The last parts of myself were dissolving with each trauma, each violation, and each loss in my young life. Year after year after year. This was my first exposure to death and it wasn't and elderly grandparent as one typically experiences as their first exposure. Losing a dear friend seemed like the last straw. Life had won. Life had beaten me down.

I was done caring about myself or others. I did not seek any counseling at school because no one could ease the pain I had endure. I was psychologically fragile already and was emotionally shutting down. I was the perfect candidate for drug and alcohol abuse during middle school and high school years. I made a decision to emotionally lock up my heart and throw away the key forever. I would replace any authentic self with a hardened persona to take its place for decades. Ironically, it doesn't really take a trained psychologist to connect the dots around the genesis of substance abuse or severe emotional and psychological problems. They typically stem from child trauma, which I have gone on to discover among my own hurting clients.

The summer after my friend's death, I experienced yet another blow. This time, something in me had changed. I no longer cared—or so I thought. I was thirteen when my brother had a friend over to the house. He was fifteen and I had a crush on him. We ended up innocently kissing, but he quickly became quite forceful. He did not stop at my pleadings. He overpowered me and molested me in the basement of our family home.

I began to panic while pushing and kicking him to get off of me. I broke loose, ran upstairs to my room, and cried on my bed. *Here we go again! Will it never end?* Later that night, when that boy was gone, I dared approached my mother again to tell her of this violation. I was embarrassed and thought I had somehow invited the molestation—as victims often do.

To my relief, my mother believed me and I didn't have to endure name callings. I would later on become mortified at the deadly consequences of telling worse than name calling. The following day, my mother confronted the boy's grandmother since he lived with her. And within one week, the boy connected a hose to the tailpipe of his grandmother's car in her garage and sat in the front seat until death took him. His grandmother was devastated, and I was horrified. I believed it was all my fault and I had caused this boy's death for saying something. Already being body/mind dissociated and emotionally numb, I just went on as best I could. I received no therapy, counseling, or adult comfort to process my profound guilt and grief.

Years later, during my own trauma therapy, I read an account from one of my heroes, Dr. Maya Angelou, about her own experience of child rape. She was speaking about her own neglectful upbringing, her mother's poor parental skills, and her lack of substantive love as a young girl. I learned that she was raped as a little girl and also reported it to her mother. Days later, she discovered that the man had been beaten to death. Dr. Angelou, then only eight years old, stricken with guilt and horror as I had been, dove into what is called "selective mutism" and stopped speaking for the next five years! She too had suffered from acute emotional trauma from believing that she had somehow caused this man's death. Like Dr. Angelou, I have carried the guilt of that boy's death for a lifetime—until speaking of it now.

As I entered high school I was adept at listened for my brothers footsteps and being locked in my room I would drown out my life to the beat of music. We were both bigger and stronger, and after spending the last decade being tied up, stuffed in closets and drawers, slapped, pinched, hair pulled, punched, molested, and generally fighting off my brother daily this would culminate into the unimaginable before my years of domestic abuse and torment would end for good. For survival, I had developed a type of sixth sense for my brother's whereabouts in the home at all times. I could sense where each of his footsteps fell and know precisely where he was. The times my senses failed me, I would end up battered and bruised. If I were caught outside my locked bedroom he would lunge at me and grab any body part he could get ahold of. And regardless of my hysterical kicking, scratching, and screaming, his menacing laughter continued. After I'd return home from high school oftentimes he'd also prevent me from getting nourishment from an after-school snack. Just when I thought he was downstairs in his room as I ran out quickly he would just "appear" and would slam the cupboards in my face, causing that ever so familiar shock of trauma sensation sending electrical shooting pain through my body due to sheer fright. Thus I went without eating many times after school.

When the violence was too much for me to bear, I would break the cardinal rule of never calling mother at work. In those days there were no cell phones and we had rotary dial. So when I lifted the receiver upstairs to call my mother my brother would pick up the phone downstairs, breaking the connection time and time again so I'd never reach her. He would laugh hysterically in my ear, and I would slam down the phone. When my mother returned from home I would plead with her like so many times before to do something about his abusive behavior, but she would just tell me I was exaggerating or give my brother a casual "knock it off." Nothing would ever really be done to protect me.

As the violence increased so did the fights. One time when I walked in the door after school, he grabbed me and wrestled me down to the ground in our living room. I was struggling, kicking, and pushing him to get off of me, but he got me in a position where he had both my wrists above my head and while he sat on my stomach to where I could hardly breathe with his weight on me he started poking my chest repeatedly with his finger and would periodically stop to produce a string of spit so it would slowly come down on my face all the while laughing. I fiercely twisted and turned my body to no avail. Exhausted, I finally gave up struggling and lay there letting his disgusting snot and spit run down my mouth and face until he was tired of getting no response. When he got off of me I went to the bathroom to clean myself up and simply went to my room and locked the door without any after-school food—again.

There was another rather violent incident in which my brother grabbed me by my left arm and with his other hand by my neck. All of a sudden I found myself being dragged into the bathroom and as I was fighting against him, he pushed my head into the toilet bowl. Into a toilet he had just used! As I was frantically trying to kick, scratch, and bite—anything to get this maniac off of me, I found my face inches from his poop! He was clearly a disturbed individual. He was a sick person with untreated psychological problems and I paid the price all my life. As all the times prior, he would eventually grow tired of his "game" and let me go.

I fell to the floor, struggling to breathe and tried not to throw up. I cleaned myself up and never said a word to anyone. I was afraid to tell my "new dad" for fear he'd actually leave my crazy family, and then I would be left alone again with no love and completely unprotected.

Another time, my brother overpowered me and knocked me to the ground in our living room. Once again as I was kicking and screaming, he managed to put the full weight of his body on my face and pass gas over and over. He was taunting and laughing again as I gagged and struggled to move my face in order to breathe until my strength gave out once more. I lay there with his butt on my face wanting to die and end this existence. His disgusting violent act left three cuts on my face from the rivets in his jeans and my neck still has problems today but like many women of domestic violence, I just cleaned myself up and went on.

The other students at school might have noticed my facial cuts but no one said anything to me and I always did my best to conceal any bruises or cuts with makeup. After all, didn't everyone have fights with their siblings? I was emotionally numb and figured I'd just carry on until I was old enough to change the circumstances myself as was my dream since I was young.

Since preschool, a good day for me was surviving another day by fighting for my life when I returned home. I was attacked one more time in high school, and I left home for good at sixteen. But not before one final epic battle that cost me my life.

It was the end of my sophomore year when I made the fatal mistake of sitting in the living room after school instead of behind my locked door in the bedroom. That day I decided I wanted to paint my toe nails, hopefully before my brother came home. I was taking off my old polish with polish remover and had opened a bottle of nail polish to begin. My brother had suddenly come home and took one whiff of the pungent smells and became angry as he said he was sensitive to strong smells. He demanded that I do it in another room—or else he growled. I had endured too many beatings over the years to know what "or else" meant. I was furious that my life was controlled by this person so when I gathered my belongings I threw back a nasty remark which enflamed his already volatile anger. In a flash, the final sibling war began. But this time I didn't care if I died, I was going to let him have as much as was in me. As I ran toward my bedroom he growled and lunged at me. He caught my left arm and began to twist it so far that I heard the tendons crackling. The tendon snapped at the elbow (I still have to wear a brace today) as he swung around with his other hand to try to slap my face but as I started to turn away to shield my face his swing caught my nose and cracked the cartilage. After so many years of violent treatment, I hated him and I snapped. I was like a hysterical maniac whose life was in danger. I felt rage for the first time and easily broke away. I was tired of being victimized in my own home.

I shoved him down and ran into my room but as I was attempting to slam my bedroom door and lock it with one lame arm, my brother put his foot in the door. I then used my right hand to grab my tennis racket and swung with all my might to protect myself by hitting him hard. I had sheer, unadulterated terror and rage. I knew my life was in real danger but I only experienced pure anger myself. I had a lame arm and a rapidly swelling nose, which made it hard to see, but I wouldn't go out of this world without a fight.

As he pushed his way in my room, I continued to violently swing the tennis racket and hit him anywhere I could to get him to stop. For the first time in my life, I did some real damage to *him*. I heard the tennis racket crunching against his body with every blow. I hit his arms, torso, and head to stop his violence. He gathered himself and came at me one last time with pure rage.

With eyes full of white-hot rage, he lunged at me, grabbed my neck with both hands and began to squeeze with all his might right there on my bedroom floor. I gasped and gasped for air, twisted my body left and right, swung my fists at him, and tried to grab his hair, punch him, or scratch him. I couldn't breathe. My throat was being crushed and as I began to lose oxygen I started to see little stars dancing across my eyes. My mind began to fade to black, and things were getting darker as I seemed to be fighting him now in slow motion.

And then suddenly I felt myself leaving my body. It felt as if I was sucked out of the top of my head. The next thing I knew, I was floating over my unconscious body. I was confused at the sight of my body on the floor but felt so warm and had a peace I had never felt in my entire life. As I was floating up on the ceiling in the corner of my room I thought to myself, am I dead? After all the years of torment did my brother finally kill me? I didn't care. I was free. I felt nothing but pure bliss and peace. I was floating above that lifeless body in complete serenity. For the first time in my life I had no pain, no terror and felt completely safe from all harm. I also felt and overwhelming sense of love, which I had never felt before. I wanted to stay in that peaceful space forever! I sensed a presence a little behind but next to me but I could not see anyone. I felt enveloped by divine, serene love. As I looked down at the scene that unfolded I could see that my brother was "white as a ghost" and he removed his hands from around my neck. Oddly, I also felt *his* anger start to subside and felt his mounting terror at the realization of what he had just done. And in a split second, as soon as I had compassion for him, I felt myself being sucked back into my body. The next thing I knew I struggled to open my eyes while gasping for breath and feeling a raging headache coming on.

With fuzzy, bloodshot eyes and a massive headache mounting I just lay there and tried to process what had just happened. My brother fiercely shook me, and when he saw I was "back" he begged me over and over not to tell our mom and bolted from my room. For the first time I saw real fear in *his* eyes. I was trying to regain full consciousness after having been completely disembodied and ethereal. Time seemed to stop and everything in my room became so surreal.

After some time I got up and went to the bathroom to splash cold water on my face. I looked in the mirror and noticed a bruised neck and several broken blood vessels in my eyes that looked hideous. I realized was going to have to go to school looking like this. I didn't bother telling anyone. There was no point after so many years. The following day I put scarf around my neck and squirted Visine in my eyes and went to high school. Decades later I was to learn that millions have reported a similar experience and it's known as having an "out-of-body" (OBE) experience.

After my OBE, I simply went on with life. That was the last time my brother ever attacked me. But the years of developmental traumas took a toll on me psychologically and I dove right into the party life of high school. Although I made the cut for varsity cheerleading I began regularly using marijuana and alcohol just to cope with my c-PTSD. I would challenge authority and get high every chance I could. I had friends who would raid their parents' liquor cabinets, and we'd drink to escape the pain of the lonely and abusive latchkey days of childhood.

It might be a foreign concept to anyone who hasn't lived a family life under that type of abuse, but there is a well-known psychological phenomenon within dysfunctional families. Many individuals experience absolute loyalty to the family regardless of maltreatment and extreme horrors. It may also be hard for many to understand, but I loved my mother and my brother very much. In my younger years I would dream of what it would be like to have a real family like I saw on TV. I also knew from a young age that my mother didn't exactly *hate* me. She just didn't know how to parent by understanding child psychology or knowing how to meet the needs of child emotional development. And didn't want to learn given the importance she placed on her career and economic necessity. I discovered from an aunt later after her passing that she herself had been severely neglected by her own mother and that the state had removed her from her mother's home for a time being placed with her with her father due to maternal neglect.

I've traced this generational theme of neglect and abuse in our family even back to my grandmother's childhood during the Great Depression. Apparently, during tough economic times her brothers were considered valued as workers on the farm and kept at home with their mother and father but my grandmother and her sister were not so useful and were just more "mouths to feed" so were shipped off to be raised by elderly and frail grandparents who were not equipped to raise young children.

I have to say however, that I am grateful every day that I wasn't raised with alcoholic parents on top of everything else. Many of my high school friends have shared horrific tales with me and my heart goes out to them. I eventually realized I could not keep going down that road of substance abuse for that would mean they had won. I wanted a better life for myself since I was a little girl. So after I got free and left home at the beginning of junior year I stopped the drugs and alcohol and attempted to be a better person. When I left home during my junior year I was finally free to become my own person—one where my past would not define me. For my senior year, I lived on my own with a girlfriend and our two dogs. I took on a part-time job to pay the rent and still went to high school. I was determined not to let my past take me down despite feelings of being damaged and not like the other kids. And so my senior year of high school began.

CHAPTER 3

The Awakening Begins

I Am Cipher

My first exposure to the world of psychology, which would end up being a lifelong love affair, began during my senior year. As the class settled in to Psych 101, Mr. Martin began the film projector showing a twenty-two-minute film called *Cipher in the Snow* by Jean Mizer. Jean had been a teacher, student counselor, and guidance director in Idaho in the seventies. This story was based on Ms. Mizer's experience as a student counselor, and the movie became an adaption produced by Brigham Young University in 1973. I found out later that the short film was later approved by the National Education Association (NEA) to show in public schools without violating separation of church and state. This startling film would change my life forever and set my life on a course of personal discovery and toward healing. But that would come decades later.

The film is a true story about a young boy named Cliff Evans. Cliff was a middle school boy who experienced the pain of profound parental neglect and a "broken home" from his parent's divorce. He was shy and stayed under the radar, choosing to become an unknown, a nobody-- a *cipher*--to his teachers and classmates. This caught my attention as an impressionable senior starting to become interested in psychology. I somehow felt a kinship to this boy's pain and loneliness. I knew what it felt like to not want to be seen.

The film opens with an ordinary bus ride to school. However, Cliff feels disoriented, sick, and dizzy. He asks the driver to be let off the bus just blocks before reaching the school. As the doors swing open, in slow motion, Cliff collapses and dies in the snow. The bus driver and students are mortified. The investigation begins and his math teacher is asked to notify his parents and write the obituary. Though listed as Cliff's favorite teacher, the math teacher sheepishly confesses to the principal that he hardly recalls the boy in his class.

I was saddened as the school counselor interviewed student after student and no one said they were his friend. And I had a bodily reaction, almost starting to cry in class when the counselor had to form a representative delegation of staff and students to attend Cliff's funeral because it was impossible to find even ten friends who knew him well. Ms. Mizer was so outraged that she wrote a powerfully moving and heartfelt article in the *NEA Journal* in 1964. She won first prize in the first *Reader's Digest/NEA Journal* writing competition. Ms. Mizer resolved never to let this happen to another child in her charge. She was steadfast in her conviction that no child in her school should ever feel like a cipher.

By the time the movie was over I knew that the study of the brain and human behavior was going to be my passion and my life's work. I was stunned. Utterly speechless. Up until this class, no one ever spoke of the reality that individuals can literally die from, not just physical trauma but can die from deep profound *psychological/emotional* trauma being perfectly otherwise healthy. This movie was shown in psychology classes across the nation to educate the upcoming generation that new research in the area of neuropsychology was indicating that chronic feelings of neglect, being unloved or rejected by society, contributed greatly to the boy's death—an eye-opening fact. I also reacted at a deeper level, feeling somehow the universe had led me to understand a little about my own tormented upbringing and how my emotional outbursts and self-harm with drugs and alcohol were the results of that chronic negative life, not "who I was" and not my fault. But this was just a glimmer of the beginnings of my personal insights, I was far from being healed.

After that day, my focus in life shifted dramatically. The study of psychology became my life. I was on a self-appointed crusade. I wanted to bring real awareness to the public of the fact that a child of neglect and/or abuse is at serious risk of spontaneously dying from a broken, lonely heart in the *absence* of physical illness. This was mind blowing for all of us in the class as we discussed the ramifications our emotions have over our health. Thus, I began a twenty-year career in neuropsychology so I could scientifically study the profound connection between the brain and the psyche.

I still had many years to travel on my own healing journey and a very long way to go after high school graduation before my own full awakening and healing. After graduation I did not immediately attend college. I was on my own and had to make money for rent and living expenses. In addition, I had only had one year away from an entire childhood of neglect and torture so I wanted to get some solid footing under me, a period of time for respite, to make a game plan for my future. Also, despite having the funds, my mother made it clear that I had to figure out a way to put myself through college. So I took a full-time job at a bank in order to save money for college. After high school, I also "discovered religion." I was ripe for religion and the Jesus movement having endured such an abusive upbringing. I thought the best course of action was to begin my journey of healing by joining a church. I told myself that at least I'd have a "faith family" where perhaps I would learn the real meaning of unconditional love and acceptance. After all, I had previously tasted unconditional divine love when I had my out-of-body experience after being choked by my brother. Christians were preaching God's unconditional love so, at eighteen, I reasoned that perhaps I could return to that wonderful place of serenity and pure love.

I was on my own finally. I had the power to take care of myself by getting the love and sense of community I felt had been stolen from me for so long. Early on, my soul had a plan for healing and I was bound and determine I would find a way to go to college to study psychology and get my college degree. I was never the same after that movie, and I had to find the answers to all my questions.

I worked at the bank until I was twenty-one when I met my husband. We were so in love, and he was my world. I really believed, being happily married now, that the worst of my life was behind me and I would have a real shot at being truly happy and having a loving family life. We both were establishing our careers early on and attempting to start a family when we discovered we were having trouble conceiving. After five years of infertility treatments and visits to the doctor, I finally conceived. We were overjoyed. But during that fragile window of time in the first trimester, sadly I was to miscarry our first child. After trying for so many years, we resigned ourselves to adoption. We planned on adopting as an alternative and had no reservations since we were both adopted ourselves. We were young and could not afford private adoption costs however so we decided to adopt a child from the state foster/adopt program. We were thrilled at the prospect of adopting a child in need and finally becoming parents. We participated in the required six-week parenting course provided by the state and began to prepare our home for the home-study visit from the social worker.

It was only after four months, while I was presenting at a real estate financing conference, that we would receive the long-awaited call and that was the longest flight home for me. I was finally going to be a mom. And I would be a *good* mom, an attentive, loving mom. I would have a family of my own and we would be blissfully happy. I had come full circle. Although I was an inexperienced, first-time parent, I had stored up years of love for this child.

After returning from the conference, my husband and I visited a beautiful nine-month-old boy in foster care who was ready for adoption due to profound parental neglect and abuse from his own biological mom. My own upbringing had taught me what children really needed: nurturing love. My heart had such compassion for this beautiful baby who had been horribly neglected in the first few months of his life that he was deemed "failure to thrive." He was an answer to many years of prayer and I wanted nothing more than to provide all the love and nurturing we both so desperately needed!

So here I was finally, in stable, loving marriage, and had adopted our first child, raising him as a Christian family. I was determined to forget the demons of my past and make my own destiny--to move beyond the neglect and abuses of my own childhood. As is typically the case, shortly after we adopted, I became pregnant again but this time I gave birth to a beautiful, bright-eyed son. I was in complete bliss having two wonderful and sweet babies. Those early days were the best years of my life. I had never known such love and happiness. I was establishing a family and building a new life with my husband and our sons.

Like many of my friends from the lonely latchkey days, I rejected the workaholic, you-can-have-it-all parenting practices of our parent's generation. My close friends and I vowed that *our children* would have at least one parent at home in their lives so they knew they were loved, wanted and cared for. We would make sure that our children had the love and attention required in child development for a healthy sense of self. We were the generation that saw the parenting pendulum swing back to stay-at-home moms and homeschooled children. The latchkey generation knew what it was like not to feel seen, heard, or loved and many of us believed we would become the generation of conscious, attentive parents by being there for our children. However, my body and mind still stored the traumas of yesteryear and would not receive the message of moving on so easily. Oftentimes my overreactions as an overprotective mother would kick in and be too much for my family, which I'll discuss more later.

It is a fact that large segments of the latchkey population, like myself, had entered adulthood, marriages, and parenting with several interpersonal and social deficits. In many ways, we were ill-equipped to raise a technology-based generation that came to be identified as the millennials. I believe there is no greater generational gap in history than that of the latchkey generation and the technologically advanced and globally connected millennial generation we raised. The electronically savvy twenty-first-century childhood—with the debut of the home computer, advanced game systems, and cell phones—was completely foreign to an entire generation whose major form of entertainment was playing outside and watching television. And unlike the early years with screen time and global connectedness through the internet that my children grew up with, the latchkey generation spent time building community friendships by playing hopscotch, listening to records, meeting up at the local swim hole, fishing, and riding bikes. My generation had a direct relationship to nature by feeling the wind and rain on our faces, having snowball fights, and playing at the beach. That grounded us to the earth. Those activities were light-years away from the virtual world of building community, friendships and relationships of through Myspace, Facebook, and real-time multiplayer gaming.

As technology entered our home I was anxious yet excited, boldly embracing this new technological future as a place for my own lasting peace. After all, we were the original Star Trek generation in which Gene Rodenberry envisioned a more equitable, intelligent, and kinder future world than the one the latchkey child was leaving behind. We thought to ourselves that this future world was upon us ad my husband and I were in agreement that we would provide our sons with early technological and educational opportunities as they became available so they would be equipped for the demands of a twenty-first-century workforce.

As parents we had always looked for opportunities to provide our boys with the very best educational and cultural opportunities for their optimal health and well-being. We were in unity and scheduled our lives so that our sons would always have at least one parent present for every activity they participated in during their school years. We were diligently present for field trips, sporting events, musical and theatrical performances, and science fairs. Much of my own inner child healing started during those early days spent rocking my babies while singing to them as the sunlight streamed in the window and later attending their elementary school events full of fun and laughter. I felt at peace in the presence of such sweet innocence and love looking up at me when my boys would wake from a nap or show me the latest frog they caught. My heart swelled with pure love and felt sensations I had never felt before adoring my time with my children.

Motherhood filled me with sense of absolute bliss and joy. Looking into my babies' beautiful eyes, I would often be brought to tears. I had never known such a deep love. I made a choice to quit my career early on and raise our children. I did not want to miss a minute of their childhood, and we both wanted to be the ones to shape their worldview with lovingkindness and attentiveness. I understand that not all women had that choice but fortunately I did and did not want my babies to be taken care of by strangers at a day care. We felt that is not why we decided to have children. We wanted to parent full time for the safety and optimal well-being of our children.

My husband and I both felt it was important for our sons to be in their own home, around their own things, for security and comfort. The rewards for me were innumerable. I heard happy babies playing in their cribs after naps and would often be met with high-pitched squeals of delight and beaming, smiling faces when I opened the door just a crack peeking at them. I wasn't about to miss that for the world.

Little did I know at the time, but in each tender-filled family moment and joy-filled experience with my children— watching them sleep, playing Legos with them on the floor, letting them stir while I made chocolate chip cookies, taking them to Cub Scout meetings to earn their badges, watching their baseball games, taking them to the orthodontist for braces, proms, or watching them graduate from high school, and year after year of watching them grow and turn into wonderfully loving and amazing young men—would begin to heal my own traumatic upbringing. My body would start to thaw and release my heart's terrorized frozen energy states.

The joy of watching, learning, and listening to my sons brought about a real and lasting change in my body's neurology and psychology, but that was only the beginning of a long journey toward my core heart's healing. My sons will never realize the many ways they saved my life and were a part of my PTSD healing journey—just like they will never comprehend a parent's protective actions until they have children of their own. They will feel that deep love that is beyond words and want to protect their child at all costs. The sweet, warm feelings of loving and being loved are foreign to many in the latchkey generation—until they had children of their own if they chose to do so. A few of my friends did not. They had been so *spirit injured* and brokenhearted, they confessed to me they were dreadfully fearful of "being like their parents" did not want to bring a child into this world. That broke my heart, knowing who they were, and knowing they would have made a wonderful parent.

For me, because of my upbringing, it was pure delight to raise my sons. I was truly smitten with a mother's love for my babies. I never regretted staying at home with my sons to guide them, love them, and watch them learn new things every day. I considered parenting the highest honor given by the God who would entrust this broken woman with these innocent beautiful babies. I felt that delightfully delicious feeling of receiving pure, unconditional love looking up at me through smiling, happy, chubby faces every day.

Although some women cannot afford it, there are a multiplicity of positive psychological outcomes for families with a stay-at-home parent. When a child's emotional needs are met at the time needed, children are more secure, relaxed, and content. They are less likely to be anxious or angry or start fights with siblings— otherwise known as acting out. Studies in child psychology also have shown time and time again that children who develop healthy, secure attachments to attentive parents during the first five years of their life feel at ease to explore the world with confidence that derives from a securely attached, grounded, and stable, loving childhood. Because I was present and able to be a stay-at-home mom, my sons and I also shared a close relationship. The boys knew I was available for them at all times, and their needs were being met, which resulted in very little sibling mischief. I kept them busy helping me around the house and in the garden as they grew, and they had little time or reason to fight. They were content and happy.

As I mentioned, many of my friends from the latchkey era were stay-at-home moms also. We formed mom groups where our children could play with other children while the moms received the community support and connection we needed. This support and community connection around the choice to be a full-time stay-at-home mom continued as my sons began preschool through a faith-based program known as "Mothers with Preschoolers" (MOPS). These parenting support communities and the friendships I made were invaluable during those early days of child rearing.

The parenting practices of many latchkey mothers had a downside however, as in any generations. Not unlike the work-outside-the-home choices of prior generations, their choices had left a lasting impression on the next generation. Latchkey adults therefore pushed the parenting pendulum and paradigm back to the opposite end from the previous generation parenting practices. From a sociocultural perspective, the "least-parented generation in history" would now generate a completely new parenting paradigm. The nineties were known for the *helicopter parent* and the *tiger mom*. The new stay-at-home movement of the nineties was in large response to being raised latchkey and an attempt to greatly minimize the time their own children would be left home alone and unsupervised. Best sellers warned about this new smothering type of parenting style in the nineties with *The Over-Scheduled Child: Avoiding the Hyper-Parenting Trap* by Alvin Rosenfeld and Nicole Wise and *Battle Hymn of the Tiger Mother* by Amy Chua.

According to the American Psychological Association, *tiger parenting* was introduced in Amy Chua's book. "Tiger parenting is a little different than authoritarian parenting in that tiger parenting includes high levels of negative parenting (e.g., strict rules) and high levels of positive parenting (e.g., warmth and support)." In March 2013, the *Asian American Journal of Psychology*, one of the American Psychological Association's journals, published a collection of six empirical papers and two commentaries that used samples of Hmong, Chinese, and Korean American parents to test the new theory of tiger parenting. The goal was to use scientific methods to test whether tiger parenting is a common parenting style in Asian families and to test whether tiger parenting leads to positive outcomes for children.

> Although there is a popular perception that the secret behind the academic success of Asian American children is the prevalence of "tiger moms" like Amy Chua, we found that children with tiger parents actually had a lower GPA than children with supportive parents. In fact, children with supportive parents show the highest GPA,

the best socio-emotional adjustment, the least amount of alienation from parents, and the strongest sense of family obligation among the four parenting profiles. Thus, our findings debunk the myths about the merits of tiger parenting. Children with supportive parents show the best developmental outcomes. Children of easygoing parents show better developmental outcomes than those with tiger parents. Children with harsh parents show the worst developmental outcomes.

My friends and I agreed however that this so-called over-parenting would still be the lesser of two evils when we recalled the sting of being left alone for most of childhood. These "over parenting" practices became the predominant child-rearing practices for the millennial generation. And whereas I saw very little of my parents growing up, my sons were inundated with "too much" of mom.

But unbeknownst to me, or my conscious mind, I was living with PTSD symptomology just below the surface waiting for any trigger to set my panic and anxiety off. One great terror I lived with on a daily basis was that somehow my dream, my perfect family, my sons, would be taken from me. I began to be tormented in a new way—internal torment—in the absence of external torment. My nightmares included images of my sons dying and it became more than I could bear.

When I had my two lovely children, I thought I was finally free from my childhood demons. I was living a wonderful life, I had experienced the tremendous joys of motherhood and was enjoying my new faith family at church. But my PTSD episodes would began to manifest more and more within my anxious mind and traumatized body in spite of all the new found goodness in my life that we had created. Like many of my clients today, I did not fully realize the extent to which my upbringing skewed my perception of reality and even affected my parenting practices.

The joys of a deep love for my husband and children was shrouded in being terrified each and every day that this would eventually all be taken from me as everything good in my life had. In my mind, I lived somewhere between heaven and hell. I was stuck in the eternal purgatory of anxiety during their childhood. When either of my sons developed a slight fever where a child's aspirin, a cold washcloth, and appropriate parental monitoring would have been sufficient, instead, it would send me into all night prayer vigils, crying and begging God not to take my babies. I was almost certain my too-good-to-be-true life would be taken from me, which again is a classic stimulus/response reaction to conditioning from my childhood. Instead of getting sleep and periodically checking their temperatures, I would stay around the clock by their sides, not sleeping until daylight and their morning naps. I would pray and watch them to make sure they were breathing until the break of dawn.

One day when my sons were older my husband and I put our youngest son on a bus for summer camp because he wanted to try his first overnight away from home. Now mind you, my boys had never been out of my (or their father's) sight and never even had a babysitter. After the bus doors closed, my husband looked at me and asked if I was all right. Apparently I was so anxiety ridden that the blood drained from my face and I was ashen white. He told me that he thought I was going to pass out. As if I willed it to the universe, we received a call that night from our son saying he decided that he did not want to stay after all. Naturally, I grabbed my coat and shoes and shot out the door and was halfway to the camp before he could say, "Bye, Momma."

In another very public PTSD episode our oldest son had to go into the hospital to have his tonsils and adenoids removed. When the doctor came to get my husband and me, telling us everything went well, they led us to the recovery room. When I discovered the nurses had let my son come out of anesthesia all alone and could see he was terrified, then saw blood all over my baby's face—my body went into full PTSD mode. I went ballistic screaming at the medical staff demanding they clean the blood of my son's face and giving them a full-blown display of PTSD hysterics. Seeing my child bloody and feeling alone among strangers had triggered a deep place in me that I was all too familiar with. So I screamed at them shouting, "All of these adults failed to protect my son's emotions so he would not be scared when he awoke!" I continued to read them the riot act. "Don't you understand the very real psychological side effects on kids who experience medical trauma? Why can't you even be professional enough to pay attention and wipe my baby's face before his own mother would see him?" I could not control my shaking PTSD episode in front of a very stunned husband and medical staff. They profusely apologized and quickly wiped my son's face but I think my outburst caused more trauma sadly.

I startled even myself and started to realize that my behaviors went far above that of even an overprotective helicopter mom! They were the reactions of an unhealthy mom. Years of my own lack of nurturing or comfort produced, in my body and mind, a pattern of disordered thinking and a level of internal anxiety that, when triggered caused uncontrollable hysterics. Those situations perfectly illustrate what behavioral neuroscientists and neuroimaging of the brain confirms: developmental childhood trauma can permanently change brain structure and functioning, thereby skewing reality and perception, causing maladaptive parenting and coping reactions.

I had another memorable hysterical post-trauma episode years later. I had been following a national news story about a young mother with two boys who were about my sons' ages. I came home one day, threw myself on my husband's shoulders, and cried, "She killed those babies! She killed her own babies! She drowned them so she could be in a relationship with a man!" My body was trembling and shaking. My poor husband, wide-eyed in astonishment, attempted to gently calm me down like a parent with a child. It would take a full week before my thoughts would stop obsessing about the dark scenes and my central nervous system would fully regain homeostasis. Again, that type of emotional investment in a stranger's children and the overreaction were direct results of own child neglect and abuse being projected onto other children. The world for me was either a battle zone of defending children or I would isolate myself and hide from the horrors of the world of child abuse that occurs on a daily basis.

Although I realized my emotional and bodily reactions to these and many more events were "over the top" PTSD also causes a type of perceptual self-blindness, in that sufferers can never fully see their reactions in proper context. My childhood traumas had hijacked my brain and changed my brain chemistry, producing psychosocial deficiencies and illogical responses to social and personal stimuli. The irrational and outrageous outbursts of my PTSD episodes, among other reasons, would eventually cost me a wonderful twenty-two year marriage. At the time, my husband and I did not understand the invisible demons I was fighting on a daily basis. I was like a veteran who has returned from the traumas of war, yet in my mind and body, I was still in the war of my childhood.

After more than two decades, I found myself divorced with two teenaged sons. After being in a long-term marriage and struggling with my PTSD, I somehow found the strength to barely hold it together for my sons' sakes, but I was sadly doing a poor job. My grief was great and my fears became a reality once again. I would go on to purchase my own home for the first time and tried my best to finish raising our sons while working full-time and pursuing my degrees in psychology.

As I tried to hold it together my PTSD attacks got worse and worse. Without the stability of a marriage, the great loss completely overtook my mind and my body. I fell into deep depression and started to feel more out of control than ever. But for my sons, I wanted to die. My dreams of having a family was falling apart.

My sons were also grieving and deeply hurting. It was too much for me to handle. I was drowning in my own inconsolable grief, and I failed to comfort my boys as they needed. I became utterly emotionally paralyzed and yet our children would pay the highest price as kids often do in divorce. All that I vowed to protect had been utterly destroyed.

I would lay in bed at night, sobbing and believing that the divorce and my grief-stricken state would be the undoing of us all. I was now actually *causing* what I had spent a lifetime swearing my boys would never experience—pain, loss and an emotionally unavailable parent. My PTSD was at its height and I regressed completely into that scared little girl. I worked and came home. I stayed in bed for hours when I could—with the sheet over my head crying endlessly. I was so emotionally bereft and lost. The powerful emotions paralyzed me and rendered me completely unable to comfort, nurture, or help my sons—even though I wanted to so badly. I believed I had utterly failed my sons from experiencing the two of the most stressful and traumatic events they could be expected to deal with all alone without a healthy parent: a broken home and a broken heart. In the early days after the divorce I also had couple of unhealthy friends who were more than willing to invite me out to happy hour enabling me to drown my sorrows. So I began drinking after work when I wasn't crying in bed to cope with my loss and feelings of parental inadequacy. But a year after my divorce, I was jolted out of my self-destructive and nonstop grieving to sober up. My youngest son began manifesting serious cardiac issues, which led me to take him to the cardiologist. I was numb inside and went through the motions still like a zombie. I felt like a failure as a wife and a failure as a parent.

As we sat in the waiting room, I looked around at the elderly patients waiting to be seen by the heart specialist and could only feel utter sadness and a deep depression knowing we were responsible for my son being here. His heart was broken from the trauma of his family splitting up—from the only life he had ever known—and like all of us, his emotional pain was manifesting itself in physically.

Takotsubo cardiomyopathy is referred to as "broken-heart syndrome," and you can literally die of a broken heart. I had seen this years before in the movie in psychology class. I had spent a lifetime fiercely protecting and nurturing my son, but where was I now? I looked around the lobby again. I wanted to hold and comfort my son so badly, but I was emotionally numb and unable to do so. Instead, I sat there with tears welling up in my eyes and wondering who would protect my sons now? There was no one present in their lives to protect and nurture them from the ones who had hurt them so deeply: their parents. I realized that we alone had done this to them. We had utterly broken their hearts—the one thing I had dedicated my life to protecting them from since they were born. Knowing we were the cause of their greatest pain was more than I could take.

I was consumed by my grief and anxiety ridden over the thought of losing my son. *After all I have had to endure in life, I could not take the death of my son!* That would have been my complete undoing, and if anything happened to either of my children, I would definitely become completely unhinged. The only true happiness and love I had ever known was that of my long-term marriage and motherhood—and I had already lost one.

The cardiologist said my son was to be fitted with a heart monitor that sent real-time data to the hospital day and night for nearly a month. He was diagnosed with PAC or premature arterial contraction, a condition that he must monitor throughout his life. With this news, I could sense my body, mind, and spirit splitting further apart. I was falling deeper into the rabbit hole of grief and pain.

Looking back now, I am thankful that the extreme pain and those events allowed everything in my life to come to a head and lead me toward my own trauma treatment. It is always darkest before the dawn, and my life felt pretty dark then. After that scare, I stopped drinking. I silently made a renewed commitment to my sons and to myself to stop running from my grief and losses, and to start dealing with the present. I would fight every demon in hell to bring me some peace and my teen-aged sons comfort once more.

I had tried far too long to hide in religion, academia, and marriage. It had all run its course, and I was left alone once more. I had nowhere to run or hide, to escape from the terrors in my mind. It was time to grow up, take responsibility for my mental health, and seek complete healing. Thus began the first phase of my healing journey—awakening my body's memories.

CHAPTER 4

Awakening the Spirit

*In the twilight of life, God will not judge us on
our earthly possessions and human success,
but rather on how much we have loved.*
— Saint John of the Cross

Like thousands of early childhood trauma survivors all over this
planet, I had an internal war going on in my mind and body all
my life and had suffered daily. Years after my divorce and having
completed my doctorates degree in psychology much of my life
looked fulfilling and successful for a Facebook moment. I had
the lifestyle—big homes, nice cars, great vacations to Italy and
Spain, and all the blessings that a life of hard work and a college
education had afforded me—but at the end of the day, it was
unfulfilling. I was empty inside.

It started to feel like I had been living a dream. I was
unconsciously going through the motions. Though studying
psychology for over decades of my life, I was not consciously
aware or even considered that my own body continued to store
trauma energies that were contained deep within my cellular
memory. Sure I knew my reactions over the years could be
extreme but thought that was just my personality given what I

had gone through. It was not until my own three day intensive trauma treatment did I fully realize the extent to which our bodies carry early childhood memories that are triggered by certain sights, sounds, and smells. These memories psychologically embed themselves into the subconscious cellular memories at the neurobiological level. When activated or triggered the body acts out—often in hysterical and irrational ways.

At that point in my life I was completely dissociated from normal sensations and messages within my body. Ever since the terror and violence of being choked forced me out of my body at the age of thirteen, I had disassociated from my body and "lived in my head," focusing on academics, facts, and being an intellectual. My mind and body became disconnected from communications because my body had never been a safe place to be in since childhood. I was only really cognizant of the memories of traumas that were severe enough to remain in my long-term memory, which is commonly referred to as *episodic memories* but denied any signals coming from my body. For example, I had an unusually high tolerance for pain, heat and cold; all signs of being disassociated and not in touch with your body's sensory messages sent to the brain. When my mind shut down however and I entered REM sleep, the body memories would come alive. Ever since I was small my nights would be filled with horrific flashbacks and night sweats. My body often tried to process the horrors of my childhood during my dreams but it wasn't enough to bring about conscious healing.

It was during this time also that I attempted to write my first book. For some reason, I could never complete a manuscript. It had always been my dream to be an author and write a book contributing my experience and education in the field of psychology specifically around best parenting practices or a how-to book for raising happy, healthy, and well-adjusted children. I just couldn't seem to progress past a certain stage. There were months when I would embarrassingly announce to my friends and family that

I was "almost done" and declare that my first book was "soon to be published" only to leave my laptop in defeat, embarrassment, and depression with several incomplete manuscripts.

Trying to analyze why I could never complete my book, I decided I had writer's block. My creative juices were not flowing, that's all, I reasoned. Somehow I needed a jump-start from perhaps another professional author. It never occurred to me at that time that subconsciously, my blocks would be related to my many negative beliefs about myself and a lack of confidence since childhood that had subconsciously kept me from wanting to be seen by others if I were actually in print. I've noticed that many of my trauma clients also engage in this behavior called "self-sabotage" which operates at the subconscious level.

So convinced I had an artistic block, and as luck would have it, I sought out a person whom I had admired since I was in graduate school for psychology and who lived "in my own backyard" in the state of Oregon. Dr. Jean Houston, PhD, is a prolific writer, psychologist, and world-renowned advocate in the human potential movement. She also lives only an hour and a half from me and periodically offers small group retreats in her home in Ashland, OR. As luck would have it, Jean was offering a retreat that summer five years ago after I decided I had a severe case of writer's block and needed help to break it.

I had admired Jean's work for years. Both she and her husband, Dr. Robert Masters had founded the Institute for Mind Research in New York to investigate the potential of the human mind. Jean's remarkable human potential work spanned decades and her research involved living with and studying the various indigenous peoples of South America. Among her many talents she would be called to the White House to offer expert counsel on Hillary Rodham Clinton's book *It Takes a Village: And Other Lessons Children Teach Us.*

I had decided years earlier that if there was ever an opportunity to meet Dr. Houston, I would take advantage of her vast experience and knowledge of both the human potential movement as well as to glean tips on releasing a creative block to become a bona fide author. I am grateful for the opportunity and Jean's help entering into the next phase of my trauma healing journey—awakening my spirit.

Everything was right on God's schedule and universal timing. The information I was to glean from the five day retreat would contain spiritual clues, moving me closer to awakening my consciousness. It was my great fortune to have spent nearly a week with an amazing small group of talented individuals at Dr. Houston's museum like geodesic dome home, which was designed by her good friend Buckminster Fuller. It would be during this time among such vast wisdom and spiritual transmission that my consciousness would be opened and expand, revealing deeper messages about where my blocks really were and what truly ailed me. I signed up for the retreat expecting a release from an artistic block but left with insights and wisdom far deeper-- an understanding into my still unhealed wounded spirit.

We may put on a good front and try to go on in life even becoming successful. We may try to fool our friends and family with a self-made persona we built over the years into adulthood, but one person we can never fool is ourselves. Deep down, the hurting can *sense* they are out of balance, out of touch, out of spiritual alignment with their authentic self. Although it may take years to put a finger on it, everyone will eventually come face to face with who they really are and who they have become. Hopefully that will be the time, as it was for myself, you shed the skin of a false self and return to your true self, free from social conditioning, free to be your unique self in this world with no apologies.

Dr. Houston had just finished writing *The Wizard of Us: Transformational Lessons from Oz,* and I was more than a little celebrity struck. I entered her home and joined the group hoping that I would experience some of her own wizardry and magical transforming alchemy. I wanted to absorb her vast knowledge and cosmopolitan energies. I imagined myself magically releasing all of my creative blocks during her retreat, returning home to write a best seller, and becoming a "real author" because of her literary artistic transmission. I may not have written a best seller but I definitely came away transformed and not disappointed.

As I attended day after day, participating in group meditation, yoga stretches, and listening to wisdom teachings, I began to be spiritually activated like never before. I began to be aware of subtle clues that were present in each activity. What the universe was showing me for my own spiritual journey was directly related to healing my past traumas rather than having anything to do with writing a book.

All the wonder, wisdom on higher consciousness, human potentialities, and comradery—to my astonishment did not come close to capturing my attention as much as one of Jean's many pets did. One cat in particular joined us each day in her living room during the retreat. All of us were initially captivated by this beautiful bobtail American shorthair who sat each day on his caregiver's shoulder suckling a blanket. The cat was well past the kitten stage, so many of us were curious as to why this older adult cat would have suckling behaviors. After a few curious comments, we were told that this cat had been a rescue cat and had suffered "tremendous separation trauma from his momma" soon after birth and before the natural weaning period. Although very healthy, loved, and well-fed, the separation trauma had *imprinted* in this cat's body so that he still felt the need to suckle and return to the blanket when feeling overwhelmed by his surroundings.

As a therapist, I was curious. Animals, by nature, cannot cognitively *remember* a trauma such as premature weaning with associated separation anxiety, and his juvenile behaviors certainly could not be attributed to all "being in his mind," as we so often attribute feelings of anxiety to humans. Where, I mused, did these suckling behaviors and separation trauma reside? The answer became clear: in the body memory at a cellular level.

I was mystically drawn each day to this cat's plight and presence. I would spend most of the teaching and silent times observing its every move and feeling a deep empathy toward him. I had felt a spiritual oneness with this feline. It was as if this cat's behavior had awoken something within me and the separation anxieties my body held as a child of neglect not having bonded as a child to any parent.

My consciousness was to awaken to the fact that I was, in fact, there to receive clues to my own spiritual healing that went far beyond any artistic block I thought I had. I started to feel a mystical, magical realm opening up and beckoning my intuition to follow further down the path. A universal spirit of love blew fresh winds into my soul and began to whisper to me. In the subtle planes I became aware of the path I must now follow toward my healing that superseded any logical reasons I had come for.

During the five days of the retreat, I became more and more attuned to the subtle realms. I started to "hear" more clearly on another level what this mysterious energy had to say. As my subtle body awakened, I made an agreement with myself to stay out of my left brain and to continue following my intuition down the spiritual path, seeking answers to newly formed questions. A most profound spiritual transformation would begin to unfold itself from past trauma and cause me to emerge out of the dark night of my soul's journey.

I returned home from the retreat no closer to finishing any of the manuscripts I had begun, but something was stirring and bubbling up in my soul that longed to be manifest. But there was also something sinister and dark that was about to surface as well from the depths of my being. Something was building in me to finally be released and was about to come to a head.

As these stirrings increased I decided I needed to isolate myself and decided to start a deep meditation practice. No one could even begin to remotely understand what I was going through trying to purge my body and psyche of early childhood trauma. I found myself alone again but this time my aloneness would become my salvation and it was all for a divine purpose. The perfect cosmic plan was about to be revealed to me through deep meditation following the next twelve months.

Meditation is a process that takes time to learn. It is not merely a matter of sitting and being quiet. Meditation involves an inner exploration of mind and body. You become the observer of your own thoughts, feelings, and emotions instead of a participant. Meditation calms the body and mind and becomes a joyful practice, a discipline, and a commitment to mental, physical, and spiritual health. It is a time for self-reflection and silent contemplation, which are essential psychological ingredients to review current and past life patterns with a nonjudgmental, compassionate mind. It is a time to self-evaluate the behaviors or responses that have served you well and determine which ones have really not served you or brought about poor results or suffering. Meditation allows space and time to examine one's life for meaning and purpose beyond a lifetime of socially conditioned responses. That is where I first placed a foothold on my own unique path of learning to calm my body, throat, and emotional responses before I could begin therapy. No one can travel that road but you.

In Eastern wisdom traditions, the beautiful lotus flower symbolizes a multilayered flowering of unfolding. Similarly, sitting in silent meditation allows an unfolding of the conscious awareness of wisdom that is buried deep within your body and soul. It can rise and teach and heal. Each time you sit in meditation, one layer at a time unfolds offering a new and deeper level of understanding of oneself—mind, body, and spirit. For me, it was (and still is) a contemplative investigation that allowed my body to calm itself and awaken to released and reveal repressed trauma messages it contained.

Along with deep breathing work, meditation allowed me to finally sense where my frozen trauma memories were stored in my body. Sitting in silence revealed to me that holding on to them was the source of all my suffering. Meditation offers many, many gifts of personal insight. For me, it was the beginning of awakening my body to begin the healing process. The saying is accurate: "You must first feel it to heal it."

Each day I sat in silence for an hour until my body revealed more and more and my soul's path led me deeper into my psyche. I expanded my consciousness, and I allowed the light of my inner being to guide me and illuminate the darkness of my terror underworld that had been so skillfully repressed and hidden from my conscious awareness for years. I had to find out why my behaviors and fears were still so dominant in my life. After all, my fears and heightened anxiety were indicative of a scared child—not an educated adult. I was ready to turn back the clock of time and call up each and every terror memory to heal this scared inner child once and for all and only my body and subconscious contained the full story. I knew I needed to fully integrate so the negative influences from my past could finally be processed and dissipate.

As my awareness opened more and more, I realized—due to the traumas I had experienced in early life and external social conditioning—I had no clear sense of self or identity. I had no self-narration. I realized that I did not know myself—and I did not truly love myself. I had been an excellent student in college receiving high marks and even authored published research. I also had a thriving private practice and was working at one of the nation's largest behavioral health insurance companies. The feedback I received from clients and supervisors informed me I was good at what I did, assisting and counseling thousands of individuals and families across the United States. Despite my many accomplishments and now healthy friends, I had never felt that I was good enough.

Ever since birth, children rely on the external world for feedback that develops or erodes our self-esteem and self-confidence. Our parents and teachers tell us how to behave and what to believe in. It is during the formative years from birth to around five or six years old that shapes our worldview and sets the stage for how we view ourselves for a lifetime. Coming from a trauma background I had a pretty low assessment of myself and my capabilities. I was also disassociated from my body and my true nature. I was, shall we say, physically present but my true inner self was not present in life anymore. It was veiled behind a trauma story. But again, revelation and awakening are the gifts of a quiet, meditative state of being that can place us on a path of permanent healing. We forget that we are human *beings* and not human *doings*. A state of being is our natural state-- a calm peaceful state where we can tap into the quantum field of energy and cosmic knowledge. It is within this subtle energy field where healing occurs in mind, body, and spirit.

As time went on, I became a more compassionate observer of my thoughts, emotions, and body messages. I became aware of the fact that I had held a tremendous amount of self-embarrassment and self-criticism in my heart. But loving silent contemplation cannot remain in a space of self-compassion and quieting the mind by listening to the body. I retreated into this sacred self-care and meditation for nearly a year prior to seeking out a developmental trauma specialist.

Meditation and yoga combined with sound therapy and aromatherapy allowed my body the time it needed to learn focused relaxation and enough time to begin to awaken deeper truths within. These mind/body/spirit practices brought me on an inner journey of questioning all my former beliefs and concepts that were woven into the tapestry of my life—the ones that were embedded deep within my psyche and body. Those beliefs were a part of me and had dictated how my trauma story played out with post-trauma reactions that I knew deep down were somehow not me. These behaviors were not who I truly was. They were learned behaviors and conditioned beliefs. Not my true nature deep within.

Silent mediation allowed space to reevaluate core beliefs stemming from childhood that belonged entirely to a sociocultural context of the latchkey era, my parents, organized religion, and American culture. I began to question how much of these beliefs and social conditioning were really me or part of my true self, my spirit, my very being of existence in this universe. It was necessary during this next phase of my trauma healing journey to question every belief I had picked up since childhood and to challenge it. I began to dismantle or pull down every paradigm and belief system that was untenable, irrational, archaic, or kept me in suffering and mental bondage—until I was fully emptied out in complete surrender to the great universal mystery of the unknown.

Each day, I could *feel* my body and mind changing at a neurological level that brought about substantive physiological changes. I began to slow down in life, scaled back on taking new clients in my part-time private practice, took many nature walks around my ten acres, started attending yoga classes regularly, changed my diet to more of a plant based diet, and started to set up healthy boundaries around who I would and would not allow in my life if they were unhealthy for me. I blessed and released unhealthy friends and ended the dysfunctional and manipulative relationship I had been in with an alcoholic who is still battling his own demons.

These healthy changes started to really build a tremendous amount of self-worth and self-confidence in me like never before. Every day I grew stronger, putting my own needs first like I had never done before. This led me to take the greatest leap of faith in my life. I decided to quit my full time job at a behavioral health insurance company. I boldly wrote a letter of resignation leaving the abusive corporate environment I had been with for over thirteen years and was now free from everything and everyone that held me back in order to grow, heal, and become all that I could be. Perhaps there are many who are reading that need to also take the leap of faith and clear out all the toxic relationships in your own life so you may become all you were meant to be.

So a year later I emerged with a calm state of mind and body with new insights about the cosmic nature of reality as well as my own true nature of being. I had gained new techniques to keep my nervous system in a calm, relaxed state while allowing my body to bring forth terror images from my past. I felt emotionally stable enough to seek out a trauma therapist. I was convinced that if I began professional trauma therapy, I would be spared the embarrassment of an acute laryngospasm attack when trying to process any unprocessed trauma remaining.

Although I was learning to live in an entirely new way and look at life from a completely different perspective, I realized that there was still more work to be done so the time was right to seek professional trauma treatment.

CHAPTER 5

Awakening the Body

Alone

Edgar Allan Poe

From childhood's hour I have not been
As others were—I have not seen
As others saw—I could not bring
My passions from a common spring—
From the same source I have not taken
My sorrow—I could not awaken
My heart to joy at the same tone—
And all I lov'd—I lov'd alone—
Then—in my childhood—in the dawn
Of a most stormy life—was drawn
From ev'ry depth of good and ill
The mystery which binds me still—
From the torrent, or the fountain—
From the red cliff of the mountain—
From the sun that 'round me roll'd
In its autumn tint of gold—

From the lightning in the sky
As it pass'd me flying by—
From the thunder, and the storm—
And the cloud that took the form
When the rest of Heaven was blue
Of a demon in my view!

The greatest factor that led me to seek professional trauma treatment was due to the fact that a life-time of repressing so many childhood traumas started to manifest in my physical health. I developed hypertension and had high cholesterol. My doctor also informed me that I was pre-diabetic and needed some lifestyle changes which began when I started my meditation practice. I knew at the time that I had the trifecta of health risk factors associated with the onset of cardiovascular disease. I was fully aware that I had all three biomarkers for a heart-attack "just waiting to happen" and in fact started to experience angina during extreme anxiety. Years after the pain subsided from my divorce, my panic attacks started to come back and occurred more frequently. Within the last few years I've ended up in full panic mode as I drove myself to the ER three times. My body was definitely sending me dangerous messages and trying to get my attention that I could no longer ignore. My body was beginning to awaken my consciousness to start paying attention to its long-repressed memories.

But dare I engage in somatic (body) based therapy? Dare I wake my body where the ghosts of my past reside? Dare I invoke the bodily memories and feelings of my brother on top of me, suffocating me, slapping me, spitting on me, choking me, tying me up—should I go back and try to process the sexual molestations, flashings from strangers or the suicide of Sam? Dare I allow those feelings of abject fright, terror and grief to resurface in my body full force once more by talking about each event in detail? Could I even feel my body anymore? Couldn't I just "get over it, move on, or let it go?" Couldn't I just meditate it away? Those terrifying feelings within my body would be like inviting death time and time again if I allowed my body to awaken fully into conscious awareness so I could process the traumas once and for all.

This journey into my past through professional help was *not* just a matter of denying and repressing memories that were merely unpleasant. Recall that I had developed also the potentially life-threatening bodily reaction known as laryngospasm. The Mayo Clinic describes laryngospasm as "a spasm of the vocal cords that temporarily makes it difficult to speak or breathe. The onset of vocal cord spasms is usually sudden in onset, and the breathing difficulty can be extremely alarming," which "can be caused from acute emotional responses." After my OBE, I developed alarming laryngospasms. My throat would seize up each time my body became extremely anxious. I soon became aware of my emotional triggers and tried to avoid certain extremely emotional situations.

I could not avoid all emotionally upsetting situations however. Once I attended my cousin's funeral. We were both in our early twenties, the same age. My cousin died of breast cancer so early in life and she left behind two small children. During the service, I started to cry. I then became hysterical, and I could feel the all too familiar signs of my throat starting to seize up and close off. I started gasping and wheezing with each emotion in remembrance of better times. I struggled for each breath. My body was in full emotional overload. I could not bring it under control.

When my laryngospasms began, I typically had to quickly find an exit to run outside for fresh air. I was desperately trying to get a breath before others witnessed my full-blown panic setting in. I was afraid I'd pass out. In addition to grief, other emotions would set off my laryngospasm. I learned to assess places and situations like closed-in spaces that might make me anxious. I tend to always sit on the outside seat in movie theaters, take the aisle seat next to an exit door in airplanes, and sit near doors at restaurants or churches in case I need to quickly remove myself during an attack.

During a laryngospasm attack, I initially try to calm my body down by cognitively assuring myself it will be okay. I then massage my throat, coaxing it to relax and open while I try to just breathe. I do my best to stop the spiraling panic that ensues from rapid throat closure and lack of oxygen. Laryngospasm is a terrifying experience. A few times the emotional overload was simply too great for me to calm my body—and I passed out due to hypoxia or a lack of oxygen.

So you can imagine that laryngospasm was not something I wanted to willingly bring on in therapy by bringing up childhood terrors again. Although many individuals suffer from cPTSD or PTSD, I've not heard from anyone who suffers from laryngospasms associated with acute post-trauma anxiety. Having worked with many sufferers of PTSD, all experience some form of bodily response however, ranging from hysterical crying to anger or rage and out-of-control shaking and trembling.

This is why it is vital for survivors of any kind of trauma to begin their recovering and healing treatments with somatic or body-calming techniques in combination with holistic based therapies such as meditation, yoga, sound therapy, or aromatherapy. The body must be in a calmed state and feel safe before it can awaken and begin to tell the trauma story. It must reveal the areas that are unhealed and in need of repair before trauma energies can be transmuted, processed, and healed. This is why cognitive-behavioral therapies (CBT) have proven ineffective as a treatment modality for trauma. A person must *feel* their trauma at the gut level to begin healing in the body.

The gut contains our "first brain" and is biologically known as the *enteric nervous system* (ENS). From a neuroscience perspective, our gut feelings are our first developing nervous system. The enteric nervous system is located throughout the lining of the digestive tract from mouth to anus and more than a hundred trillion neurons reside there. It is not the brain but the stomach that produces more than 90 percent of the body's neurotransmitter (serotonin).

Differing from the central and peripheral nervous systems, scientists have discovered that our enteric nervous system can actually function independently of the central nervous system (CNS). When the ENS was completely cut from communications with the CNS in one study, neuroscientists discovered that electrochemical messages can still be sent and received via the enteric nervous system directly to the brain—independent of the central nervous system. Why do I bring this up? Because it is the ENS that has also been referred to as our *intuitive nervous system.*

It is for this reason that many parents of young children teach their child to listen to their gut when feeling uncomfortable in a situation. Many parents teach their children to trust their guts (messages from the ENS) upon meeting strangers to nurture this more intuitive and more accurate sixth sense of neurochemical information system for self-guidance and discernment. These parents understand child development and know their advanced cognitive abilities of higher-order reasoning for logical discernment don't come online until around age ten. It is still beneficial for all of us to remain open and aware of what our gut is telling us for our mind/brain can trick us.

After a year of committed silent meditation and yoga practice I felt I had reached the deepest parts of my trauma body memory as a little girl that resided in my gut and was able to drop deep into that gut place of awareness with self-tenderness and compassion in order to *feel* the earliest (and youngest) messages of my childhood trauma. In my gut, I started to feel biological energies stirring for the first time since a child as I saw images of myself as a terrified little girl with no parental comfort. I had great compassion and I felt what she felt and saw how that little girl inside was still so terrified of the dark, of storms, and being murdered or kidnapped even as an adult. I had feelings of someone watching me at times, waiting to grab me. I began to understand that the primal areas of my body still contained these traumas--illusions of shadowy artifacts, left over terror memories that were imprinted in my body during the times my brother would appear out of nowhere and grab me.

So with tender compassion and skillful expertise Dr. Julie led me through a yearlong somatic-based therapy program that would radically change my entire physiology and state of being. During therapy I started to get real relief from my lifelong sufferings and emotional dysregulation. I fully realized that the body—not the mind—contains the process by which to deeply heal. Continuing with my meditative practice we began with a primary component to approaching any trauma treatment-- vagal nerve stimulation.

Many trauma experts and behavioral neuroscientists, including myself, believe the Vagus nerve is the key to health and well-being. The vagus nerve is one of twelve cranial nerves (CN X) and is located in the brain stem. It relays information directly between the brain and the craniosacral organs. Vagus is Latin for *wandering*; therefore, this nerve is also referred to as "the wandering nerve" that affects all organs of the body system. The vagus nerve is part of the parasympathetic nervous system within the autonomic nervous system, and it allows individuals to calm down or regain bodily homeostasis after a stressful event or trauma.

Essentially, my nervous system had to learn and unlearn. More specifically, it had to be repaired and rewired. During vagal stimulation sessions, I could feel my physiology changing in my mind and my body. After a year of hard work, I learned a completely different way of being and thinking. The old trauma neuronal pathways were rewired and repaired by my brain's ability to form new neuronal connections (neurogenesis or plasticity). In doing so, an entirely new world opened up to me.

Dr. Julie had skillfully assisted me in processing many of the feelings I had repressed, but we had come to a point where she was concerned I still had not fully allowed that little girl within to let it all out so it could be fully transmuted and processed. And what she meant by that was any remaining deep-seeded anger. I had always been the "good girl" wanting everyone to like me and never to upset the apple cart. This stemmed from classical conditioning of wanting to be good enough for mother to love me and never upsetting my brother to provoke beatings and torture. Therefore I had never really been able to fully express my anger at what had been done to me, ever. Until now.

Each session became an "ollie, ollie, oxen free" in which I would imagine that frightened, neglected, and tortured little girl and allow her to come out and be seen and heard. I allowed her to speak and feel within a space of compassion. I could access the images and feelings of an inner child who still felt abandoned, lonely, and cut off from humanity but had a difficult time visualizing and more importantly, allowing that angry darker side of the inner child to come out and be expressed. To be honest, I was terrified to let lose my deep, seething anger against the injustices that had happened to me. I didn't feel I had a right at this late stage of the game. I argued that I had moved on and did not harbor any deep seeds of anger but Dr. Julie knew better.

She and I both knew the danger of repression is that if we do not allow ourselves to fully express our darker feelings even among safe and compassionate persons they eventually become expressed in our mind and body in the form of depression, anxiety, chronic illness, and disease (dis-ease). So in more than a few sessions I allowed myself to get angry!

I became angry—angrier than I have ever been. The trapped energies began to flow through my soul like lava bubbling up. I spewed rage against every abusive and neglectful act perpetrated upon my younger self. For the first time, I allowed myself to be really angry even at God. I wanted it all out! I charged life with being a cruel joke and heaven with being cruel taskmaster, allowing little boys and girls all over this planet to be treated with such neglect and abuse. My anger seethed and boiled up to meet the pain in my heart. I was spiritually throwing up all the toxins in my body and soul. It demanded to be released from my body, from this earthly realm where such cruelty and hate resides between human beings. What was I to learn from this? I was angry at pithy loathsome remarks such as "what doesn't kill you makes you stronger" or the even more insipid and ignorant comment of "your challenges and hardships are what makes you the person you are today." I held nothing back.

Like Lt. Dan in *Forrest Gump*, I would shake my fist at God and challenge Him asking: what sense did these seemingly senseless spiritual lessons make when shrouded in a hall of mirrors within the mind that are nearly impossible to navigate, but heaven remained unmoved. My anger turned to madness, and my depression deepened. I was completely undone and left in a spiritual black hole. There is one saying that is true in my life however, "it is darkest before the dawn" and my life at that point was at its blackest. But my coming breakdown would be my breakthrough!

In the final month of my trauma treatment I rarely got out of bed. I had stopped seeing clients, family, and stopped all socializing. I was alone, unemployed and on the verge of bankruptcy. I was completely exhausted in mind, body, and spirit after one year of intensive psychosomatic trauma work. I was completely emptied out and in deep depression with residual anger lingering. I was literally fed up and done with the struggle of this thing we call life and I wanted to "go home." I had overcome so many horrific things in my life, raised a family, put myself through college, had a thriving private practice but did not want go on anymore. Years earlier, I had gotten a glimpse of the spiritual world when I had an OBE when my brother choked me out and I wasn't scared in the least to return to that place of unconditional love and feeling of safety. I knew I would once again feel the overwhelming power of love emanating from the Source once more, and I welcomed it. I had run out of answers and did not care to analyze anymore.

As I lay in bed one day and felt the warmth of my tears slowly rolling down my face like so many times before, I try to will my breath to get shallower and shallower. I decided to finally surrender to the sadness and depression. The years had taken its toll on me. As I could feel my heart beat slow down and my breathing become shallow, I thought, *I will just surrender fully to the mysteries of life and death.* I started to feel my heart shuddering with arrhythmia and grabbed my chest in pain. Even as I took more and more shallow breaths, I was not afraid. I was resigned and just surrendered. I felt my time had come. I wanted this. Life would go on.

As I stared at my ceiling, paralyzed with sadness, my breathing seemed to stop. I was once again out of my body but this time I felt myself slowly rising up to the ceiling with my arms outstretched in the same position I had been on the bed. As I rose, the ceiling became translucent and what appeared before me were galaxies with millions of glistening stars embedded in a backdrop of black space.

This time, my out of body experience was very different than my experience decades before in childhood. This time, I felt my ethereal body and not just a consciousness as before. This time, I also sensed more than one being, I felt the presence of five or six entities or beings all around me as I slowly floated into deep space. There was complete silence but there was also that familiar feeling of unconditional love enveloping me in the blackness of space as I lay floating amongst the Milky Way. Time stood still. In fact, there was no meaning of time in this place. I was peaceful and serene once more.

As I was floating, a celestial vision unfolded before me as I was witnessing millions upon millions of stars and swirling galaxies all around me. I was unafraid. The beings, perhaps angels, perhaps my guardian angels, did not speak, but I felt their immense unconditional love and presence all around and through me to my very soul.

I strained to look into the starry night, hoping to head home to the light so many speak of who have had a near death experience, but it was made known to me that I was in a place and a space of healing, compelled by these light beings to remain until their work had been completed. Still floating, I turned my head to the right and saw something that looked like a black, starry curtain that was slowly pulled back to reveal my entire life played out like a movie in an instant. I was shown my life from birth, adoption, raising my sons, to present day. From the traumas to the joys. I also was shown where I had made emotional choices that kept me bound but where I could have brought myself out of my trauma pain and suffering sooner had I made another choice. There was no judgment, only learning.

I was also shown times I had hurt people badly myself and other times I chose to love and show kindness and compassion instead. In this life reviews I actually *felt* what that friend, person at the store, or family member felt when I hurt them and yet also *felt* the times I showed compassion and love from their perspectives. It was like I was in a play, experiencing all the emotions of the actors at once. Again, these beings showed me my learning opportunities throughout my life without judgement. I was experiencing the power of the words, gestures, and negative energies we hurl at each other so thoughtlessly. Far beyond what we realize, they caused deep wounds or tremendous blessings and healings. I felt the impact of my own words as they caused deep emotional wounds and pain to others, but I was happy to also experience the little things I had done to make a difference in others' lives. By simply showing kindness and compassion to children and adults, my acts of kindness had changed the course of their paths in life. These beings continued to show me more about my life. I saw where I had great opportunities that were opened to me but because I clung to my trauma story they had passed.

At that moment, it was known to me the deeper meanings of all the holy texts throughout the world, that we alone hold the power to crucify or resurrect people by our words and actions. We greatly affect their minds, bodies, and souls on this earthly plane by choosing who to love or hate. We pick and choose who to give love, hope, and compassion to and who to hurt, hate and withhold love and compassion from. We alone hold the power to change the world by changing ourselves. This is the wisdom of the universe and of the ages.

I understood how I had held tightly to my brokenhearted feelings and my trauma story for years. Yet I also broke others' hearts with my unkind actions. They continued to show me that the choices and actions toward others we think are insignificant are actually all recorded in the celestial (or *Akashic*) records for our learning after transitioning from this earthly dimension into other dimensions that are more real than this world. There was no hint of condemnation from the five or six celestial beings that surrounded me as I learned these truths about the course of my life. As these being were floating serenely around my entire energy body, and I recalled a verse from the Bible that refers to "ministering angels." A deep feeling of unconditional love continued to press in on my energy body and surround me. These beings then gave me, for a lack of better words, a type of "download" in my consciousness or mind—a kind of mental transference of universal understandings of the true nature of reality and how everything had its place and purpose in this existence. I thought of another scripture I had remembered speaking about "*all* things working together for good."

After the review of my life and the download of the true nature of reality, as opposed to how we view our own subjective reality, I somehow understood my place in this world for once. And how I could not die, it wasn't my time. How every individual's life had meaning and was important and how deeply everyone is loved. Somehow, I also understood the entire quantum energy field of connectivity, like Indra's bejeweled energetic net spoken of in ancient Tibetan texts, which connects all sentient beings to each other.

In this suspended plane of existence, I could see the ethereal energetic threads that connect us all to each other on this planet. Like strings on a violin, if the vibratory field of one is struck, it sends a vibratory ripple effect across the planet in the unseen quantum realms. I knew in an instant that we are all one and are connected in the energy field of consciousness. The actions we perform on one another ripples out like waves on an ocean of cosmic consciousness to affect the whole of humanity. I was shown the oneness of everything and everyone and how we are all individual expressions of the divine light of love incarnated in a human body. We are not separate from each other in the quantum realms because matter is merely made up of vibrating energies as quantum physicists are reporting. Like individual flowers, bright and lovely; they are individual, yet all are connected at the root.

There is but one energy or vibration (what many call God) where all beings emanate from. There is one light or source—the divine Creator—or cosmic mind. The Logos, or the primordial sound om, whatever you choose to call it, that brought all things into existence and holds all creation together by the vibratory field of Love. It transcends all religion. Hate and evil are located in the hearts and minds of men and women who are trapped in own their stories. They play out their pain on others. It does not emanate from the one universal, eternally unfolding, unconditional expression of divine love.

I had no idea how much time had passed on this earthly plane, but after my life's review and the celestial download—in which vast amounts of information were transferred to my very being in what was likely a nanosecond—I felt a female being or angelic presence floating softly right up to my face. It seemed as if she was hovering over me with an indescribable glistening robe and loving smile. I understood then that this place was a healing place as she placed her hand on my heart, and I felt an intense wave of healing energy. It was like if you stand too close to a bass speaker, I felt a vibrational wave that seemed to vibrate from the energy field of my subtle body down into my physical heart as my physical body was still laying on the bed.

I felt no pain whatsoever. Instead, it felt like a vibrational wave of pure divine love that produced a celestial healing. I felt as if my broken inner child's heart had finally been repaired and made whole by a divine, energetic vibration of love in the quantum field. It was a lovely, peaceful feeling which has never left me to this day. It was like stepping into a warm bath. I knew instantly I was changed forever and I would never be the same again. I was a completely transformed person. I honestly didn't know if I was dead or not, but I did not want to leave that place of healing and pure love. Before I knew it, I was back in my body once again. As I came back into awareness of this world, I opened my eyes slowly and saw through new eyes with new understanding and a heart full of love for myself and the entire world.

As I wondered what I had just experienced in the spiritual realms among the stars, planets, and galaxies, I had another experience, I began to taste lilacs! In neuropsychology, this condition is known as *synesthesia*. A person can experience neuro-perceptual crossovers among any two of the five senses.

Nobel Prize-winning physicist Richard Feynman reported seeing equations in color for example.

The taste of lilacs was still in my mouth as I heard a whisper. It said, "Your heart is healed from this day forward." In an instant, I was fully awake and aware of my surroundings, but I did not want to move or disturb the sweet healing peace I felt within my spirit. It had finally awoken to all things true. I was in such a deep state of bliss—from the top of my head to the bottom of my toes—that I could not deny what I had just experienced. I was so different. I could tell. The vibrational energy of the celestial healing in my heart was like a permanent energetic imprint that had healed years of trauma. The depression, sadness, grieving—all was gone.

In the following days, my mind attempted to trick me. I thought I had experienced a grief-stricken, depressive hallucinatory dream, but the following days and weeks and now years confirmed the reality of my permanently changed heart and what had taken place.

After weeks had passed, I wondered to myself, *What about the sweet lilacs I tasted?* I instantly knew the beings of light and love had given me a personal gift as a symbol of the alchemical process of healing love. For it was because the first time I left my body was due to horrific trauma--in the lilac city. And so it was, the second time I had left my body it was to be healed and awaken my childlike heart so I could live my life to the fullest and freely forgive all those who had hurt me while I was growing up. I knew beyond a shadow of a doubt what I had experienced was truly finished and forgiven. My heart was healed from that day forward just as I had heard in the whisper on the wind.

In 1975, Dr. Raymond A. Moody, Jr. coined the phrase "near-death experience" in his best-selling *Life after Life*. I have discovered, since my experience that thousands all over the world have reported similar experiences even under the conditions of medically recorded clinical death in which they "went to the light and experienced unconditional love." The testimonies are unique but similar to my experience as well. Many souls have returned from the other side to tell their stories and give their testimonies. At the time you wonder if you are crazy or had hallucinated but since my experience happened thankfully I discovered the International Association for Near-Death Studies (IANDS) were there are more than 193 medically documented cases on IANDS's YouTube channel. I feel no embarrassment about coming out for the first time and telling the tale of my traumatic early start in life or my soul (or consciousness) twice leaving this earth plane to experience celestial healing among the stars and loving beings.

Since my healing experience, I also was delighted to come across the work of Dr. Ebner Alexander MD, a neurosurgeon who, after his own near death experience, wrote the book *Proof of Heaven* and has now let go of his classically trained Western medicine dogma stating that humans are no more than biological machines and consciousness does not survive death. Current dogma states that the brain's neuroanatomy somehow generates our consciousness, although no neuroscientist can explain how. Dr. Alexander and hundreds of other physicians, nurses, hospice workers, and laypersons alike from all around the planet are coming forth and offering their OBE/NDE testimonies that will hopefully one day warrant more studies and perhaps overturn the dominant paradigm and challenge all dogmas.

Like Dr. Alexander and thousands of other around the world, when you have had such an experience you realize that death is merely an illusion and that we do not die. You understand to your core that we are eternal beings having a human experience. When we drop the body, we merely return and go home to the pure cosmic and divine love that is eternal.

We, as a planet, are waking up. I've yet to meet a person who is *not* sensing, at the subtlest levels, that global change is coming. Many former archaic and dogmatic control mechanisms will collapse. We are witnessing a new age. This change is not to be feared. Western medicine can no longer deny or turn a blind eye to the thousands of medically documented cases of individuals dying and their consciousness leaving the body only to be revived and recount with great details what they saw and experienced. Many individuals are given the choice to reenter the body to fulfill their purpose on earth.

Since my experience, my entire life has changed. Having lost all fear of death and dying, I had a strong desire to serve others at a local hospice and began volunteering for bedside vigil. I am fulfilled when I offer love and compassion to those in transition to the other side, holding their hand and speaking words of comfort. After my experience I somehow feel at home comforting the dying and their bereaved families, assuring all that there is no reason to fear death and reminding them that our loved ones are still with us, for they live in spirit just as plainly as you and I are living now on this side. I am happy and alive like never before! I no longer chase status or success and live a heart-centered life that has allowed new doors to open, new friendships to blossom, and have been offered new exciting opportunities to serve others.

Letting go of my lifelong trauma story has freed me to be in service to others in need, among loved ones and within my community. I now work with others struggling from PTSD related to childhood traumas, counselling individuals on best parenting practices, and offer spiritual coaching. I am finally the captain of my soul!

Invictus

William Henley

Out of the night that coverd me,
Black as the pit from pole to pole,
I thank whatever gods may be
For my unconquerable soul.
In the fell clutch of circumstance
I have not winced nor cried aloud.
Under the bludgeoning's of chance
My head is bloody, but unbowed.
Beyond this place of wrath and tears
Looms but the Horror of the shade,
And yet that menace of the years
Finds and shall find me unafraid.
It matters not how strait the gate,
How charged with punishments the scroll,
I am the master of my fate,
I am the captain of my soul.

Dear one,

If you or someone you love is acting out in a way that you feel is over-the-top reactionary, please have kindness, patience, and love and consider that they might be experiencing post-trauma symptomology and are unable to control the neurophysiological mechanisms that compel them to act out. For more information on receiving expert therapy for developmental trauma, contact me at www.growinguplatchkey.com or email at drdarlaphd@gmail.com to schedule an in-person or Skype counseling session.

Many Blessings,
Dr. Darla

For further educational resources for living with or loving someone suffering from PTSD for either veterans of war or childhood war, I highly recommend the following books:

- *The Body Keeps the Score* by Bessel Van der Kolk, MD
- *Healing Trauma* and *Waking the Tiger* by Peter A. Levine, MD
- *Healing the Child Within* by Charles L. Whitefield, MD
- *The Truth about Mental Illness* by Charles L. Whitefield, MD
- *Life After Life* by Dr. Raymond Moody, MD PhD
- *Proof of Heaven* by Dr. Ebner Alexander MD
- *God and the Afterlife* by Dr. Jeffery Long MD

Also, if you—or a loved one—are having suicidal thoughts, please reach out and seek help immediately! Call any number below if you feel there is no hope left but to harm yourself. There is *always* hope for complete healing! You are loved. I love you.

National Suicide Prevention Lifeline (800-273-8255)
Youth Line (877-968-8491)
Veterans Crisis Line (800-273-8255 press #1)

CPSIA information can be obtained
at www.ICGtesting.com
Printed in the USA
FFOW02n2113240518
46865561-49099FF